Bears Repeating
Stories Old Teddy Bears Tell

By Terry & Doris Michaud

Illustrations by Thomas J. Mocny

Published by Hobby House Press, Inc.
Cumberland, Maryland 21502

Additional Copies of this book may be purchased at $14.95
from
HOBBY HOUSE PRESS, INC.
900 Frederick Street
Cumberland, Maryland 21502
or from your favorite bookstore or dealer.
Please add $1.75 per copy postage.

ISBN: 0-87588-263-3

Table of Contents

Dedication

This book is dedicated to the memory of the late Peter Bull, who reawakened the love and sharing that is within all of us.

Acknowledgements

We wish to thank all of those people whose contributions have made this book possible, including the following: Pat and John Schoonmaker; Dennis and Melody Adomaitis; Len and Jane Servinski; Jean and Bill Lawson; Peggy and Alan Bialosky; Alison, Greta and Jim Gibson; the hundreds of shop owners, friends and strangers who have helped our antique Teddy Bear family grow; and the Teddy Bears whose stories will have to wait until next time.

"Thank you" to Gary R. Ruddell for his faith in us, and to A. Christian Revi for his guidance and patience in working with two people who knew what they wanted to say but didn't quite know how to say it.

A very special "thank you" goes to a very special and talented photographer, Tom Mocny, a business associate, confidant and personal friend who truly knows the meaning of giving.

Finally, we must say "thank you" to our children Mary, Patty, Jim, Terry Lee and Kim, for allowing their parents the freedom to remain in their second childhood.

Terry and Doris Michaud

OPPOSITE PAGE: *A treasury of antique Teddy Bears in the parlor.*

Foreword...

Foreword...
The Carrousel Shop And Teddy Bear Museum

Chesaning, Michigan, is a small village comfortably located in central lower Michigan less than an hour's drive from Lansing, Saginaw or Flint. It is just this small town atmosphere that attracted the Michauds to the community. Frequent visits to see their daughter and her family educated the Michauds to the benefits of living in Chesaning. A beautiful Victorian mansion on the Boulevard came on the market, and the seed was planted.

It seemed ideally suited to locating a shop and museum covering the entire first floor, with ample living quarters on the second and third floors. This Chesaning landmark was built in 1895 by the first doctor in the village. It is the kind of home that dreams are made of, with beautiful oak floors and woodwork throughout. Plumbing and wiring had been updated by previous owners, but the beauty and charm of this truly unique Victorian home have been preserved.

Excellent timing was another major factor in relocating the Carrousel operation to Chesaning, as a number of beautiful old homes on the Boulevard were being converted to quaint shops. The community is experiencing a rebirth that is attracting tourists and visitors from all over Michigan and from neighboring states.

LEFT: The Carrousel Shop and Museum, a beautiful 1895 Victorian home in Chesaning, Michigan.

OPPOSITE PAGE: *One of two ornate fireplaces in the living room.*

And Then There Was One

To tell you the story of the Carrousel Museum Collection of antique Teddy Bears is an exciting and somewhat overpowering assignment, but one, I must admit, I am probably uniquely qualified to do. To begin with, I was actually the very first Teddy Bear acquired for this now famous collection. Add to that the fact that my background is deeply rooted in academia, and it becomes obvious that the honor of telling this story rightfully rests in my hands (or paws, to be perfectly correct).

Alas, I cannot be too specific about my background, for it is my fate (as it is with so many of my kind) to be forced to accept that aura of mystery concerning my origin. As best can be determined, my date of birth is set in the 1915 era, and it is strongly suspected that my roots are German. I cannot state that I originated with the famous Steiff family, for there not only is a lack of a button in my left ear, but there isn't even a trace of a darkened hole where it would have been located. It would be personally comforting to know that my origin could be positively traced to the Hermann family, makers of truly excellent Teddy Bears for many years. Perhaps some day a geneologist who specializes in tracing Teddy Bear trees will solve the mystery, but meantime I am content to know that I was greatly loved by my original owner (a

fact attested to by the well worn mohair on my body), and I am equally as loved today as *numero uno* in the Carrousel collection.

Now, about that academic background. I was discovered by Terry and Doris Michaud at an antique doll show in Holt, Michigan, in 1972. Holt is a suburb of Lansing, which is adjacent to East Lansing. East Lansing is, of course, the home of the world famous Michigan State University. It is perfectly logical to speculate that perhaps I was the cherished object of some famous German scholar who came to the Univeristy to obtain his PhD in Languages, or perhaps in Music. The poor soul may have passed away without a family to pass on his posessions to, which would have included me. After the usual long and tedious court proceedings, I was likely sold as so much excess baggage, along with the late Professor's other worldly goods. One thing that is known, and that is that it was love at first sight when Terry and Doris spotted me lying half upside down in a cardboard box under an antique dealer's table at the previously mentioned doll show.

"How much for the old worn bear?" Terry inquired.

"Twenty Dollars" was the reply as the dealer cautiously sized up his potential customer.

"I'm a dealer, and I'll go fifteen" Terry stated after a quick glance toward Doris, who's eyes sparkled with approval.

"Oh, I guess there's not that much interest in Teddy Bears, so you've got a deal" the doll dealer responded.

True, it was a very good buy, particularly for someone as esteemed and intelligent as I. But you must remember that there was a great deal of truth to the dealer's statement about the lack of interest in Teddy Bears.

I suppose the fact that I only had one ear may have had some influence on the price. It was a rather embarrasing situation to me, and I tried to keep a cap off to one side so it wasn't quite so

LEFT: Deadlines, deadlines! Doesn't Chris Revi know that even bears have to rest?

OPPOSITE PAGE: The Professor in hand knit sweater, gold wire rim glasses.

noticeable, but laying upside down in a cardboard box caused my cap to fall off, so the decision to take me home by the Michauds had to be strongly based on love. I didn't know it at the time, but Doris had the needed surgical skills to correct this matter of a missing ear. The logical approach would have been to find some matching mohair and make a duplicate. Come to think of it, any mohair is difficult to find, let alone finding something to match. But Doris is as clever as she is skilled, and she remedied the problem by removing my one good ear, and carefully removing the thread holding the two pieces together. Thus, a front and a back became two fronts! Then it was a simple matter to find some closely matching material and creating two new backs to go with the two old fronts. From all outward appearances, I am now a whole and complete Teddy Bear.

You would expect that my name was naturally chosen because of my acquisition so close to the home of Michigan State University. I must confess that the name came about in a rather strange way. Terry and Doris spirited me home after their for-tunate find, and showed me off to the family. Their daughter Kim (then 8 years of age) took one look at me and exclaimed,

"Why, he looks just like my teacher. He even has cat hair and dandruff on his sweater!"

Although not totally kind, her remark was received so favorably by the Michauds that, from that day forward, I have been known as "The Professor." With my black knit sweater, rumpled plaid bow and wire rim glasses, I am perfectly content with the title. My likeness has been adopted as the Carrousel logo, and every handcrafted Teddy Bear made by the Michauds carries a tag with my portrait on it.

It is a point of pride with me knowing that I founded (or caused the founding spark for) the Carrousel Museum Collection that has been hailed by many authorities as one of the most significant collections of its kind anywhere.

Even though my personal story must remain primarily speculative, there are many Teddy Bears in this collection that have factual stories to share. And we shall share them with you now.

The Professor admires a beautiful contemporary Teddy by artist Elaine Fujita Gamble.

The Librarian

Living by the principle that a collection is only of value if it is shared, the Michauds' schedule of lectures and public appearances continues to grow. It can be difficult to find time for such activity in the demanding world in which they live, but find time they do. This sharing and caring attitude is recognized by their audience, and has resulted in the acquisition of some of the most treasured Teddies in their collection.

We had the pleasure of appearing with Terry and Doris on a TV talk show in Michigan, in 1977. Many of the bears were shared with the audience, but with my academic background, I must have

had a strong impact on one viewer, because shortly after the program Doris received a phone call from this wonderful lady, who said she had a Teddy Bear she wanted to send to them.

"That's great," exclaimed Doris. "Is it an old Teddy?"

"Well, it was mine, and I'm Old!" came the firm, but friendly reply.

After an offer by Doris to stop by and pick it up, the lady said she would simply mail it. Several

BELOW: *Yes, we have a great number of books about Teddy Bears.*

anxious days passed, and after what seemed like an eternity, the mailman brought a package to the Michauds' door. As tempting as it was to rip it open, Doris set the package aside until Terry returned home. He came through the door and barely had time to get his coat off when Doris thrust the package into his hands. Like children at Christmas time, the box was quickly opened to reveal a thin, 12in (30.5cm) Teddy with sparkling shoebutton eyes peering out with some apprehension. He looked a bit forelorn, but obviously well loved. Tucked in the package along side of Teddy was this heart-warming letter from the owner:

"Teddy was born in 1909 and given (to me) at birth. He was just a beloved toy and then a friend and confidant all through high school, Lake Erie College at Painesville, Ohio, where he received his A.B., and then at the University of Michigan where he received his M.A.L.S. (M.A. in Library Science.)

"I think he came from the toy department at Hawley's Store (now Knepps). Long ago there was a little silver trademark disk in one ear (note hole) but I have long since forgotten what it said. Maybe just 'trademark.'

"He's been hugged and kissed and wept on and loved these many years. I now entrust him to you, who sound (like) just the right person."

The letter was signed by the lady, and it was several minutes before Terry or Doris could speak. I must admit to being equally as moved, but I couldn't wait to tell the Librarian that we were practically classmates! It mattered little that his school and mine were strong rivals, located some sixty miles apart, and that his date of graduation preceeded mine by six years. We hit it off immediately, and I was able to introduce him to the rest of the gang and ease his apprehension coming to a new home.

Another wonderful Teddy joins the Carrousel Museum family.

Paddington's Forebear

The search for Teddy Bears is included in all of the Michauds' travels, including business trips, vacations, or a weekend shopping trip to a metropolitan area. Terry and Doris have developed an ability to turn up Teddy treasures on paths that have been well worn by others, probably due in great part to years of dealing in antique toys and dolls. They are seldom swayed by the statement that "it's a waste of time to look for Teddy Bears in that area." In fact, the statement becomes the challenge and catalyst for the hunt.

An anniversary trip to England and subsequent revisits have given Doris and Terry the opportunity to add some very significant bears to this collection. Any of the usual tourist-type attractions are fitted in around plans to attend antique markets, shows and antique malls. Looking through the touist guidebook listing of street markets produces a variety of activities grouped by category, such as "London's leading fish market," or "a weekend vegetable market popular with the locals." An inquiry about one such listing assured the Michauds that it would really be a waste of time, because the market was made up of fish and poultry stalls, and "street after street of vendors selling new clothing." Scheduled the same day is the Petticoat Lane market, and it is promoted as "the market where the dealers shop" — it seemed an easy choice. Following the "early bird" theory, our two eager bear hunters were on the scene at six o'clock on a Sunday morning, early enough to catch the dealers as they set their merchandise out for sale. After carefully and thoroughly making the rounds of all the stalls at least three times, the tally showed one toy and two nondescript composition dolls, but alas, no Teddies. It was now 10 A.M. and after a hasty conference, the decision was made to check out the poultry market.

If nothing else, this market certainly was colorful, with hawkers dressed in attention-getting garb, waving hard-to-resist bargains at every turn. Intermingled with poultry and fresh fish stands were row upon row of clothing stalls, winding through many blocks of streets and alleys.

Late afternoon arrived, and our duo tired of pushing through crowded streets of new merchandise. To get away from the crowds they took a sidestreet that led to a block-long complex of antique shops covering two floors. Now most of the shops were closed that Sunday, but with little else to do, the Michauds decided to check out each and every door. On the second floor, they found a shop filled with furniture and glassware, and as Terry glanced through the doorway his eyes fell on a very large bureau whose top was covered with Teddy Bears! Better yet, the owner was there "just doing a bit of tidying up," and the door was open.

An inquiry brought forth the information that the shop owner was a "Teddy sport," and had that very morning decided to "weed out the collection." She had a total of eighteen she planned to part

This 1920s English Teddy does some research on a modern bear that strikes a remarkable resemblance!

with, and only a financial limitation prevented all eighteen from returning to the states. Ten of the better bears in the group did make the trip, including one that the Michauds have decided just has to be Paddington's forebear. This 10in (25.4cm) Teddy from the 1920s wears a wool coat and pants, and a heavy knitted sweater was found under the coat. The hat, secured with an oversize hat pin (ouch!) gives him the perfect appearance for his role as Paddington's forebear. This English Teddy predates Paddington, but he certainly epitomizes one of England's most popular characters. One has to wonder if this bear was seen by Michael Bond and served as an inspiration.

Because of his character and charm, this bear almost always gets to go on display with the traveling Carrousel Collection, and without so much as a formal introduction, the most frequently heard comment is "I see you have an early Paddington!" He may not be a direct descendant, but one could not hope for a more charming kindred spirit.

OPPOSITE PAGE: Forebear is well prepared for a cold day in London.

BELOW: *Today's English Paddington and his Forebear?*

The Sweet Smell of Success

The Michauds owe a debt of gratitude to many people who have contributed to their successful hunt for Teddy Bears, including a host of friends in the antiques business. These associates frequently seek out Terry and Doris at shows to share a recent bear find, and more often than not it ends up in the Carrousel Collection.

When setting up for an antique show, the Michauds are always torn between getting their merchandise out and on display, and making the rounds of other dealers in the never-ending search. They usually take turns at both assignments.

At one of their regular mall shows several years ago, Terry was "making the rounds" when one of the dealers hailed him. She said she had just the item for their collection of bears.

"I've got a Teddy Bear that a hundred dealers have tried to buy from me" she said, "but I just wouldn't sell it. But it really belongs in your collection."

"What is it?" Terry inquired.

"A perfume bottle" came the response.

"Gee thanks for thinking of us, but I'm really not in to perfume bottles" Terry responded, visual-

With head removed, the Perfume Teddy Bear exposes the glass container which originally held a ground glass stopper.

izing a flocked bottle in the shape of a bear.

"Now, don't make a snap decision until you see it" admonished the dealer. "I'll bring it in to the show tomorrow."

Next day Terry was making the usual rounds, half forgetting the offer, and as he approached the lady's booth, a small brown bag was pulled from under the table and thrust into his hands.

"Check this out while I take care of some customers" the dealer said.

Terry opened the bag and removed one of the most sought-after Teddy Bears ever produced, the earlist version of the perfume Teddy with ground glass stopper. It was in mint condition, and Terry's heart was pounding as he waited for his friend to return.

"Still not interested?" she chided him.

"Never again will I say no without seeing the merchandise" Terry said, with wallet in hand. After paying for his new treasure, he mumbled something about having to get back to his booth, and had to force himself to keep from breaking into a dead run to show Doris the prize of the show.

Left: 3½in (8.9cm) *Perfume Teddy with original stopper.* **Right:** 4½in (11.5cm) *Perfume Teddy.*

Getting Lost & Other Good Things

Traveling through the State of Indiana on their return to Michigan one summer, the Michauds got off the expressway for a lunch break. This was one of those exits that does not provide an entrance to return to the freeway heading in the same direction. An inquiry was made at the service station next to the restaurant, and Terry received clear, concise directions, followed by the inevitable "you can't miss it." You can in fact miss it, and they did. A turn to the north here, a swing west there, a few blocks in this direction, and lo and behold! Lost again!

Terry was mentally rehearsing a speech he would give to the attendant at the service station, when a sign caught his eye, and all thoughts of mayhem passed on as he pulled the car to a stop.

The weathered sign, not much larger than the lettering on it, read "Antiques" and stood at the edge of the road next to a small shop that originally served as a garage for the adjoining house.

The shop was small but pleasant, and there were a few collectible toys and a composition doll that were picked up by Doris and carried to the sale counter. Terry found the shop owner to be a very pleasant and inquisitive lady, and since he only needs an audience of one, Terry proceeded to tell her about the Carrousel Teddy Bear Museum collection. He described some of the keystone Teddies in the collection, including the rare perfume Teddy. He went on to say that they hoped some day to find the companion piece, which is the equally rare compact Teddy.

A puzzled expression came over the woman's face, and resting her chin in a cupped right hand, she said "why, I believe I had one like that when I was a child. If you have a few minutes, I'll go take a look." "Lady, we've got all day," Terry assured her. "Good. You mind the shop and I'll be right back," she said as she briskly headed out the door and over to the adjoining house.

After what seemed like an eternity, but in fact was more like twenty minutes, the shop owner returned clutching a well worn but extremely rare compact Teddy. It was bereft of all of its mohair, showing only the pink backing of the original covering. Removing the head, Terry slowly slid out the brass cap that held lipstick in its day, and parted the torso which was hinged at the back, to reveal a powder chamber and mirror inside. Trying to appear casual at such a moment can challenge the most practiced Arctophile, but Terry managed to remain calm, keeping a locking grip on the treasure, as he raised the usual question regarding sale of said Bear.

"Oh, I couldn't possibly sell it," said the woman, and Terry felt a sinking feeling in his stomach as he told the lady he understood her sentimental attachment to the Compact Teddy. "That's got nothing to do with it," she retorted, "It's in such terrible condition I just couldn't ask any money for it!" It took a moment for Terry to regain his composure, but he then assured her that even in its poor condition it would be a welcome addition to their collection. And it is, indeed.

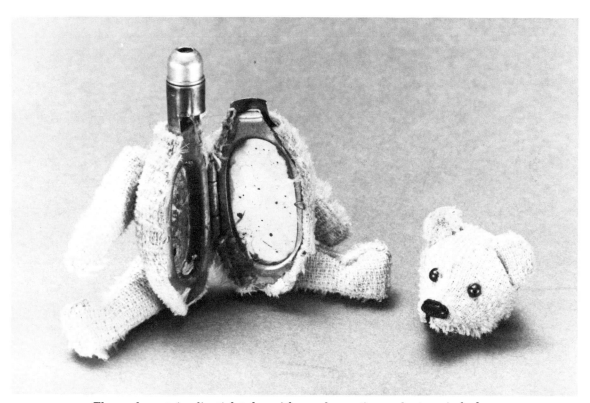

The neck contains lipstick tube, with powder section and mirror in body.

OPPOSITE PAGE: LEFT: *A Teddy Bear Compact joins forces with an early perfume.*

OPPOSITE PAGE: RIGHT: *3½in (8.9cm) of well worn pink mohair.*

Peter

My title of the "First Teddy Bear" in the Carrousel Museum Collection is undisputed. I would also like to feel I am the most loved, the best looking, and the most valuable, but I'm afraid I could be challenged. The most valuable would certainly find Peter as a major contender. He is one of the rarest bears in our group, and one that the Michauds discovered in England. While making the rounds in a very large antique mall, Terry poked his head into the open doorway of a shop that obviously had nothing to offer in juvenilia, but our intrepid couple learned many years ago that Teddies sometime take up residence in the most unlikely places.

"Any toys, dolls or Teddy Bears?" Terry asked.

"Nothing of that sort," came the friendly but positive response. As Terry turned to move on to the next shop, he was hailed by "Wait a minute! I did purchase two Teddy Bears last week from a gentleman from Germany who claims to have found them in a warehouse over there. Would that be of interest to you?" The bears had been taken home by the dealer, who likely felt they were out of place in his shop of exquisite crystal and furniture. Arrangements were made to return the next day, and an anxious twenty-four hours passed.

Shortly after opening hour, Terry and Doris walked into the antique shop and reminded the owner of their interest in his recently acquired Teddy Bear.

"Oh, yes. You came to see this," he responded, handing the bear in his original box to Doris.

Doris removed the cover, and gasped in amazement as Peter stared up at her. Terry smiled and reached for the wallet of traveler's checks as he inquired about the price, knowing full well that Peter would be coming home with them.

While this amazing Teddy Bear would never win a prize for warmth and cuddliness (a bear term), he is most certainly rare. The story of finding 100 Peters in a German warehouse has since been confirmed. He has flirting eyes of the type found in antique dolls, and they move in conjunction with his movable tongue, which protrudes from an open mouth. I can tell you that my fellow bears and I have been noted for our expressions of love and tenderness, but I'm certain that Peter probably scared the tar out of some child.

Each bear stands 14in (35.6cm) tall. They were made in Germany by Gebruder Sussenguth in the middle to late 1920s. The label on the box has an illustration of a Teddy Bear, and states that the box contains a "bear with the most nature-like finish."

The supply of these rare Teddies has long since been consumed, and the Michauds have turned down offers of many times their original investment. It is interesting to note that the late Peter Bull also had a "Peter" bear in his collection for a time, but he told the Michauds that he had to trade it off as it "scared the dickens out of the rest of the bears."

LEFT: Label on original box.

OPPOSITE PAGE: *Peter has shaded brown mohair, with wooden eyes interconnected to a bisque tongue, allowing movement. 14in (35.6cm).*

There Are Teddy Bears, And Then There Are Teddy Bears

If you think Teddy Bears are popular now, you should have been around back in my early days. We bruins were so popular that we made an appearance in many forms beyond the traditional Teddy. Teddy Bears were imprinted on anything that could take an imprint, including scarves, articles of clothing, dinnerware, children's metal tea sets, and hundreds of other items of bearobilia. (I'm not sure you'll find that word in Websters, but as a Professor I feel I can take journalistic license.)

Teddy made an appearance in many forms as well, including porcelain and bisque figures, hand carved wooden Teddies, jewel-encrusted bears, crystal, blown glass and anything that could be shaped, bent or sculpted in the image of dear Ted. Not surprisingly, the handcrafted mohair Teddy also took a variety of forms. There was the Teddy Girl (another story we'll deal with later), Teddy bodies with a bear face on one side of a plush head and a doll face on the opposite, and Teddy Bear heads on a sack-like body that served as a bottle cover.

One of the more popular items that every young lady felt the need to include in her wardrobe was the Teddy muff. Now, for those who spent their entire life in a warm climate such as one might find in Phoenix, San Diego, or some other equally delightful and warm locale, you may have a bit of a problem identifying with the need for a Teddy muff. However, those among us who have felt the biting cold of a Michigan February can fully appreciate the comfort afforded the proud wearer of a Teddy Bear muff.

Unfortunately, they were only found in little girl's wardrobes and would have been considered

Teddy Bear Muff in excellent condition. Circa 1918.

much too sissified for a young man to wear. I'm not in a position to tell you when the simple hand muff made its debut, but doubtless it was before the turn of the century. I can tell you that adding the Teddy Bear to this article strongly enhanced its appeal and charm, and soon Teddy muffs were being worn (and proudly so) by literally thousands of young ladies around the world.

It is difficult to come across examples of this popular form of Teddy, so you can understand Terry's increased pulse rate when, at the St. Charles Toy Show which they attend with regularity, he spotted a fine Teddy muff in mint condition that had just been unpacked by a dealer. Alas, a rather portly gentleman was standing next to the table between Terry and the Muff, requiring a rather awkward bend and reach that might remind one of the second stages of brake dancing. When a sharp glare by the man caught Terry with an expression of being discovered with your hand (or paw) in the cookie jar, Terry dropped the prize and mumbled something like, "Sorry, I didn't realize you were dealing on it," and walked away feeling more disappointed than embarrased.

Another twenty minutes brought Terry to the last booth in this particular building, so as he turned to head for the door he decided almost impulsively to make one more pass through the booth where he earlier discovered the muff. Much to his amazement and delight, the muff in question was still perched on the table. The time it took for him to secure this treasure in the tight grip of his hand would be difficult to measure, but it surely could be rated in nanoseconds (a billionth, I believe). "Didn't that gentleman want this muff?," Terry queried. "He surely did," the dealer responded, "but he spent all his money for toys and just couldn't come up with the money." Having already checked out the price tag, Terry was comfortable in stating, "Well, it's sold now."

It did take a bit of convincing to sell Doris on the idea that their collection simply wasn't complete without this speciman (a true statement), and that peanut butter and jelly sandwiches spread out (parden the pun) over a month's time might help to offset the already offset budget. Normally a discussion as to the advisability of a purchase takes place between Terry and Doris, but every once in a while a treasure turns up that is simply not going to be set back down on the dealer's table. The Teddy Bear muff was such a treasure.

Over Pricing And Under Pricing: Dealer's Choice

Let's face it! Antique shop owners and dealers cannot possibly be authoritative on every single item that crosses their threshold, particularly if it is an item that is not directly related to their specialty. The cut glass dealer may know little or nothing about old jewelery. Yet, he will occasionally buy a collection or an estate, and he finds himself in possession of something out of his realm of knowledge. He can either seek information as to its value, or he can price it according to what he has invested in it.

More often than not, dealers will tend to overprice an item about which they know little, based perhaps on the fear of selling something for less than it's value. Usually they conclude the price is too high after the item in question has gathered dust in the shop for a long period of time, and the price is adjusted accordingly. Then there is always the dealer who is not so concerned by market value, but determines a price based on his cost plus a fair profit. It is from this type of dealer that the occasional bargain is acquired.

While browsing through a large antique mall in southern Michigan several years ago, the Michauds discovered no less than six Teddy Bears in various stages of disrepair and price ranges. Five of the six were from the 1910 to 1930 era, and in poor condition. Mohair was more noticeable by its absence, soiled and torn fabric was common, and an occasional eye and/or ear was missing. Now I would be the last Teddy in the world to suggest that a fellow bruin with an ear missing has no value, particularly if the potential buyer has the talent to mend the situation — if you'll forgive the pun. However, one must realize that as with any item of antiquity, Teddy Bears should be valued in direct proportion

Lucky boy? Lucky Bear! He's part of a well loved, frequently shared collection.

to their condition. A Steiff Teddy Bear in mint, unplayed with condition will have far greater value than a Steiff with all the mohair worn away, both eyes missing, and an ear gone, particularly if the missing ear contains the prized button!

Now, where were we? Oh, yes. Most of the Teddies at this antique mall were on the down side of poor, to say the least. However that did not daunt the dealers from affixing price tags to them that would more properly belong to mint condition bears. Number six, however, was a different story. Here we have a very beautiful fully jointed Teddy of about 1930s vintage in pristine condition. His mohair was longer than typically found on bears from this era, and more importantly, it was a cinnamon color not commonly found. Apparently this led the dealer to conclude that this Teddy was of a later vintage, for the price was extremely low for such a prize.

Needless to say, Teddy was delivered to the check-out counter at the front of the antique mall, where an exchange of funds took place without the usual price haggling. The Michauds' calling card was placed in the hands of the clerk with a parting comment, "Call us if you get any more like this."

At the same mall a box of early starched collars was found, and the newly acquired Teddy insisted on wearing one. Gives him the look of a storekeeper of days gone by, don't you think? This Teddy Bear is an 18in (45.7cm) example of an American made bear from the 1930s, very likely a Knickerbocker, from comparison with similar known bears. Collectors are always pleased to find a Teddy in unplayed with condition, but I get a little sad thinking that such a bear never enjoyed the love and attention that I did. Love worn adds a special dimension that speaks for itself.

The Knickerbocker Teddy has long, curly cinnamon mohair. This 1930s Teddy is 17½in (44.5cm).

Reginald From Rye

Some people will do absolutely anything to acquire a Teddy Bear. As a bear, I can certainly understand that, because we do tend to be very lovable creatures. But I'm not sure all humans understand this overpowering desire.

Take, for example, the time the Michauds were touring England in a motor car. Terry was behind the wheel, and from what I have been able to gather from Doris and their daughter Kim, it was a rather hair raising ride (mohair included) since it was the first time Terry had driven on the left side. I do accompany the Michauds on many of their travels, but this is one trip I am rather grateful I wasn't invited. He did have a note attached to the dashboard that said "think left," but old habits are hard to overcome. They tell me the worst moments were coming out of or into a turnabout, or a circle at the intersection of two or more roads. Add to this confusion the need to watch every sign and shop for indications of antique shops, and therefore potentially Teddy Bears. It's no wonder that daughter Kim and her friend Gayle Kinney suggested on more than one occasion that returning to London might be a lot of fun.

The touring group of four made a stop in the small English hamlet of Rye. Two things prompted this stop — it was getting near lunch time, and Doris spotted an Antique Shop. This is going to be a good news, bad news story, the good news being that said shop had a most attractive 10in (25.4cm) British Teddy ensconced in the center of the shop's front window. The bad news was the sign in the door that stated the shop was closed on Mondays. I need not tell you what day it was. Terry did everything but stand on his head to see the price tag, but it was positioned so that it was impossible to read it, a habit, I might say, is all too prevalent in antique shops.

All through lunch Terry and Doris talked about what a marvelous little town this was, and how nice it would be to spend the night there. Kim and friend Gayle had already resigned themselves to the fact that the first two people in line when the antique shop opened its doors on Tuesday morning would be two Americans from Michigan. Indeed they were, but the bad news was not completely told, as Terry picked up the bear, only to discover that the tag read "Not For Sale!" It seems the proprietor had been newly bitten by the Teddy Bear bug, and felt that by placing this bear in the window it might bring in some additional bears. The bear was hard to resist, due perhaps in part to the fact that he was wearing a red velvet tam that gave him a special charm.

Undaunted, Terry explained their primary mission in England was to acquire fine bears for a museum in the United States, and that they had in fact spent the entire night in this hamlet specifically to acquire this particular bear. This would signal many a dealer that a handsome price could be obtained for the item in question, but this lovely English lady was finally persuaded that the bear would indeed have a happy home, and she put a very reasonable price on him. Reginald now spends happy days with many of his countrymen (countrybears?) in Michigan.

A 10in (25.4cm) British Teddy Bear well worth waiting for.

Our mechanical Schuco shares the spotlight with a German celluloid 7in (17.8cm) doll, and a tin Parcel Post truck from the turn of the century.

From Germany to the U.S.A., by Way of Holland

On their 1985 Southwestern personal appearance tour, Terry and Doris kept a hectic schedule of appearances with the antique bears from their collection, introducing their new handcrafted bears, and doing an occasional toy, doll and bear show. It was their first opportunity to be a part of the Glendale Toy Show, one of the largest shows of its kind in the country, and probably the most popular toy show on the West Coast.

Arriving at the auditorium just a half hour late, Terry found a lengthy lineup of dealers waiting to check in, and as he waited impatiently, he visualized all the great Teddy Bears being grabbed up by other dealers. Sometimes the excitement of the moment causes him to overlook the certainty they concluded years ago that if they were meant to have a particular bear, it would be waiting for them under any conditions.

Moving their boxes of merchandise into the auditorium to their assigned space, the Michauds discovered the dealer at the next table was from Germany, and his entire table consisted of stuffed animals by Steiff and Hermann. They gladly helped him unpack the overflowing boxes and managed to restrain themselves to a limit of about a dozen pieces. They were a nice lot, but did not include that special piece that quickens the heart beat.

There were over 200 dealers at the show, and only a few hours to see the selection and get set up (in that order, of course). The doors would open to the public at 10 o'clock, and it would require at least 45 minutes for our dynamic duo to put their merchandise out, even though they had limited themselves to one table for this show.

The first hour had passed all too quickly, and now it was time to get the table ready. But wait! What's that little bear over there with the red tam on? Is it? It is! It's a marvelous 5in (12.7cm) mechanical Schuco, standing there with arms outstretched, waiting for someone to turn his key so he could perform. This booth, located diagonally across the little room where the Michauds were set up, was operated by a young man from Holland. His entire booth offered a variety of tin toys, some rare and most expensive. The only bear he had to offer was the little Schuco. His English was somewhat halting, but he had no trouble in explaining the United States dollars he had to have for the bear. In spite of the rather hefty price tag, Terry certainly didn't want this young boy to have to lug this bear all the way back to Holland. Must be the kind heart in him, don't you think? At any rate, the exchange was made, and it made the show for the Michauds. The bear sports red felt pants with leather belt, and a red felt tam with black tassle. When wound, a vibrating action causes him to dance and spin around on his metal feet.

Teddy dances to this music of an organ grinder from his era.

The 5in (12.7cm) mechanical Schuco greets the Parcel Post truck, a tin windup from the early part of this century.

Her Teddy Lives On

Some of my fellow Teddy Bears in this collection have glad stories to tell, and some have sad stories. When the Bears are on tour, Terry usually tells the glad stories, and Doris ends up with the job of telling the sad stories. Since I am the spokesbear in the printed media, I'm afraid it's my duty to tell you a sad story.

The Teddy Bear we're speaking of is a beautiful gold mohair Teddy that dates to about 1915. He is a rather large Bear, measuring a full 22in (55.9cm). His origin is believed to be American, perhaps an excellent example of one of the famous Teddy Bears made by Ideal Toy Corporation in their early years. The condition of this Teddy is pristine, with one minor exception, due to the fact he was hardly played with.

The Michauds received a phone call one day back in 1974 from a lady in Bay City, Michigan, a short distance from their residence of that time in Midland. She said she had been told by a friend that the Michauds had an interest in old Teddy Bears, and she was calling to confirm this. She had just inherited her Aunt's estate, and had just returned from a trip to Ohio to inventory the belongings. Packed away in a steamer trunk was a Teddy Bear that originally belonged to her cousin.

Arrangements were made to pay the Lady a visit within a few days, and when Doris and Terry saw this Teddy, they knew it was a very special Bear. Doris marveled at Teddy's wonderful condition, but noted that the left paw had been repadded.

The woman reflected on the comment for a moment, then unfolded the sad story that explained why the Teddy showed few signs of wear. "My cousin played with this bear almost constantly, carrying it by the left paw. Her mother covered over that paw, and I'm not sure if it was worn, or if she wanted to keep it clean. At any rate, when Susan was seven years old, she was playing on their front porch one day, and she fell over the railing and fractured her skull."

The room fell silent briefly, for by this time neither Doris nor Terry were capable of speaking. "I suppose my Aunt could have given the Teddy Bear away, but somehow it got put up in the attic and didn't come to light until we went through her belongings," the lady said. She told the Michauds that she felt good about the fact that it was now going to someone who would appreciate it.

This is one of a select group of Teddy Bears in the collection that gets to tour with the traveling collection, a special honor accorded but a few of us bears (including me, of course!)

Teddy contemplates a happier time.

Game time, as Teddy finds a friendly partner.

An excellent example of an early American Teddy, 22in (55.9cm) of dark gold mohair.

Second Hand Rose

Adomaitis Antique Shop in Saginaw, Michigan, is owned and operated by Dennis and Melodye Adomaitis, two warm and outgoing young people who really care about the goods of yesteryear. More importantly, they really care about people, and this is reflected in their efforts to assist every customer, whether they are purchasing a complete service of china, or a simple button hook.

Their specialty is vintage clothing, and much of their stock comes from purchasing entire estates in the Saginaw Valley. This area has a rich history from the Victorian era, when lumber barons lived in palatial mansions throughout the region.

It was in such a mansion that Second Hand Rose turned up. Everything had been carefully put away in the attic of this beautiful home for many decades, and as Dennis and Melodye made their way from front to back, they discovered to their amazement that as each layer was uncovered, it was like going back in time. They went through an inventory of goods first from the 1960s, then the fifties, forties, and right on back to the turn of the century. An old shoe box was removed from a steamer trunk, and the graying cord was untied to allow removal of the lid. Staring up at them from its hiding place of many years was a mint condition mohair jointed Teddy Bear with turned up nose. As far as the Adomaitis' were concerned, this wonderful 16in (40.6cm) Teddy Bear had the Michauds' name on it, and a phone call the next day gave them the news.

Second Hand Rose pauses in her busy day.

It is difficult to judge who was the most pleased, because when Terry and Doris were introduced to Rose, Melodye was smiling as broadly as they were.

When Rose came to the Michaud residence, she was a "Bare Bear" (a term commonly used to refer to us Teddies when we are found without benefit of costume). However, sometimes it becomes obvious that a particular outfit is appropriate, and this was certainly the case with Rose. The Michauds manage to keep an inventory of doll clothing, and after searching through several boxes, Doris came up with a tiny red leather purse, a felt hat and a genuine fur piece, complete with glass eyes, clamp jaws and a tail. Velvet ribbons and feathers for the hat completed the ensemble, and now this wonder-ful Teddy would forever remind the Michauds of their friends Dennis and Melodye, and their love of vintage clothing.

Soon after the bear joined the Carrousel Collec-tion, she was being shown to an admirer. After she was told the story of how she was acquired, she asked if the Michauds had come up with an appro-priate name. When she learned that the bear was as yet unnamed, she said it was obvious to her that she should be called Second Hand Rose, and she has been so called ever since. An added discovery is that her squeeker works, but very faintly, which gives her a soft, gentle voice befitting a Victorian Lady.

The Estate is gone, but the memories linger on.

Lights! Camera! Action!

While my particular talent lies in writing, which would, of course, be expected of a professor, there are many other talented Teddy Bears in the Carrousel Museum Collection. We can't all be authors, but since most bears have at least one unique quality, we can each take pride in our individuality.

Some of my fellow bruins are unique in size. The Duke of Portobello towers over most of the gang, while tiny Debonair Bear (under 1in [2.5cm]) can hide himself in the Duke's curly mohair! Other talents amongst the group include two perfume Teddies who can remove their heads to allow access to a body filled with the lovely fragrance, and yet another who's body opens to reveal a hidden compact.

I could go on and on talking about many other talented Teddy Bears, but the group that holds the greatest fascination for most people visiting the Museum (and I confess many of us Teddies as well) are the bears known as Mechanical Teddy Bears. As with many titles, it can tend to be a catch-all phrase, but basically it applies to those bears who have a mechanism activated by either a windup spring or by battery power. We could, of course, include such delightful Teddies as the Feed Me Bear who operates under people power, but for the purposes of this story we will stick to the key wind Teddies.

One of the oldest in the group (probably from the 1920s) is a tumbling bear made by the firm of Schuco. Since we have already given him recognition earlier in the book, we'll simply mention that from a collector's standpoint he is certainly ranked with the most desirable.

Equally as old but originating in another part of the world is our circus performer, a marvelous Teddy that spends his days tightly gripping a large wire hoop that he stands inside of, and with just a little coaxing he will do loops across the floor with the greatest of ease. He is referred to by toy collectors as Paper Label Japan, which means he at one time was identified by a paper label and was produced in the 1930s. Another wonderful performer that falls into this category is our Roller Skating Bear. This show off does very large circles on his oversize shoe skates, and half way through his large circle he will do a series of smaller circles.

Perhaps not as old, but certainly great performers in their own right are the group of windup Teddy Bears that were produced in Japan in the 1950s. This was a great era for windup and battery operated toys of all kinds, but of particular interest to the arctophile are the talented Teddies that seem to have no end to their antics. In our group you'll find a sweet lady bear who continually knits, another young female who powders her nose, and one of Terry's favorites, the bear with glasses who spends his entire day wiping them clean and trying them on. That's one talent I could use, instead of having to depend on a human to do it for me.

Once in a great while, late in the night after the Michauds have retired for the evening, we coax a few of our performers into an impromptu act. It doesn't always elicit a response from Terry or Doris, but the family Dog Brodie reaches a high state of excitement I can assure you.

LEFT: 4in (10.2cm) Schuco Tumbling Teddy.

OPPOSITE PAGE: Show Time at Carrousel!

1930s windup from Japan.

Paper Label Japanese roller skater from the 1930s.

4in (10.2cm) Schuco Tumbling Teddy.

Getting A Head
(But Just Bearly)

Teddy Bears can turn up in unusual places under the most unusual conditions. Or is it, unusual Teddy Bears can turn up...Oh, well, no matter. This particular bear fits the description no matter how it's worded.

A very large antique market takes place twice yearly in Midland, Michigan, that covers the larger part of the county fairgrounds. Dealers are attracted to this event from many states, and since the Michauds were based in Midland during the developing years of the Carrousel Museum Collection, it was a market they checked with regularity. Sponsorship of the market by an organization of devoted old car buffs meant that there would be row upon row of rusty fenders, crankshafts and other automotive parts of varying age and condition. By far, however, were neatly arranged rows of tables of antique and collectible bric-a-brac. Who can judge when an item crosses the threshold from yesterday's junk to tomorrow's treasure? Sometimes these markets attract a much larger propensity of flea market merchandise, but this particular market was much closer in fact to its title of antique market.

Working one side of the row of tables while trying to keep an eye on the tables on the far side can be a little awkward, but the knowledge that another great find is out there waiting to be discovered keeps our two friends in hot pursuit. A glance to a far table revealed the classic outline of an early Teddy Bear torso, partially masked by a cardboard shirt box sitting on top of it.

As he quickly made his way toward the target area, Terry noticed that this bear was a most unusual red color. It was indeed an early jointed bear, with grey felt pads and a short mohair body. The next thing he noticed that made him increase his gate slightly was a rather large piece of masking tape stuck to the left foot, and a black felt tip pen marking, showing the price to be $10.00! Grasping a leg and holding up the bear, Terry said, "I'd like to

Restored 1913 Steiff Bär Dolly. 16in (40.6cm).

buy this ...... bear ... body," his voice trailing off with obvious disappointment as he discovered that the bear was headless. However, years of experience in dealing with antique and collectible dolls taught the Michauds that even parts had value and were worth acquiring, so without hesitation he reached for his wallet and produced the required ten dollars. The thought that maybe a matching head would turn up some day passed through Terry's mind, even though the odds of this happening were probably comparable to winning the Irish Sweepstakes.

The bear body was placed away in the brown paper bag the dealer placed him in and all but forgotten, until the Michauds made a trip to the New York Toy Fair in February of 1984. This is a large market of wholesale suppliers and manufacturers who offer the newest toy and doll merchandise to the retail trade. While in the Steiff showrooms, a group of postcards showing early Steiff bears were reviewed by Doris. A bright smile crossed her face when she turned up a card that showed a group of early Teddies — including the red bear! Even more of a surprise was the discovery that this 1913 Teddy named Bär Dolly had a beautiful head of white mohair, set off by an orange yarn ruff.

This discovery inspired Doris to dig through her supply of set-aside pieces of material until she came up with some white mohair. She then designed, cut, sewed, stuffed and finished a replacement head for Bär Dolly. Constructing a yarn ruff like the original completed the project.

A head transplant is scheduled for some unknown future date when the original head turns up, but meanwhile Bär Dolly is content to sit on his assigned shelf in the museum, clutching the postcard that inspired the restoration project.

Is headectomy a proper term? Hmmmm. Better check that one out.

BELOW: *Bär Dolly discovers an early picture.*

The Old Man

Asked by a newspaper photographer during an interview to hold his favorite Teddy Bear, Terry replied "I'm not sure I can hold that many!" Certainly with such an excellent selection, it would be difficult at best to choose a favorite, although I must admit I really expected to be a top contender. After all, I was the favorite son before all these other bears came along. In all fairness, I don't think I'm loved any less. I'm more inclined to believe that the Michauds have such a huge capacity for loving Teddy Bears that as each one comes along that capacity simply expands like gas in a container.

If Terry were somehow forced to pick one all-time favorite, it would be the bear he calls "The Old Man" because he was so touched by the man and his story.

The Teddy we're talking about came to the Michauds early in their collecting avocation, back in the late 1970s. They were in the second day of one of their regular antique mall shows, and apparently I had captured the attention of someone the previous day with the sign I held that read "Wanted — Old Teddy Bears." It was late in the afternoon when Terry looked up to see a gentleman of advanced years approaching the booth with his Teddy snugly nestled under his arm.

An early Steiff Teddy in rare cinnamon color.

Goodness! It's almost time for tea and honey.

"Wanna see my bear?" the old man inquired, holding it slightly aloft but firmly in his possession. "He's marvelous!" exclaimed Terry, "Did you want to sell him?" "Nope," was the immediate response, and returning the Teddy Bear to the security of his arm, the man strolled away.

The gentleman's wife, who had been standing back and listening to the discussion, stepped forward. "He really does want to sell it, but he can't talk about it," she said, and she went on to explain that an overly active dog in the family had been causing some bad dreams about Teddy meeting his demise, and a safe, secure home was enough motivation for the old man to part with his beloved companion. A short while later, the lady returned with the bear.

The Old Man, as Terry calls the bear, is an early Steiff in a long, curly mohair of rare cinnamon color. The glasses were added by Terry, who feels they remind him of the original owner. The Michauds learned several years ago that the gentleman had passed away. When Terry shares Teddy Bear stories with audiences, you can be sure that The Old Man is proudly given his moment of glory.

BELOW: The Old Man stands 19in (48.3cm) tall, but prefers to sit.

Two Out of Three Bears

One of the interesting challenges bear collectors face is the identification of an acquired bruin. The Michauds operate on the premise that if you ask enough people and show the bear in question to enough collectors, someone will come up with an answer. Too bad they don't seek my advice. I could certainly be a great help in their search. I guess it's the old story of the answers being right at hand.

During a trip to California in 1982, Terry and Doris had the opportunity to attend a toy show in in San Jose. Many of the toy shows and doll shows of a few years ago have now incorporated the Teddy Bear name and theme into their shows, but that is a more recent development. We Teddy Bears were not always as popular as we are now. But no matter what the show may be called, they are usually ideal hunting grounds for the arctophile.

BELOW: *Waiting for Papa to come home.*

By 1982, Teddy Bears were starting to command respectable prices, and they were appearing at these shows in greater numbers. This toy show was no exception, and a plentiful supply of Teddies were at hand, sporting what seemed at the time to be rather high prices, thus creating the usual game of taking enough time to see everything that's offered, but not too much time so as to miss out on that first bear that caught their eye. Terry claims to have a rule that, "if you like it, if the price is right, buy it," but even he wavers at times. A lovely lady bear caught the Michauds' eye on a shelf, and it was taken down for closer examination. Lady bruins are quite rare, you know. Oh, I don't mean the occasional Teddy that under protest has been outfitted in a pink pinafore or has had a lace collar wrapped around his neck (oh, the indignities we Teds must endure to keep our humans happy), but rather a Teddy that has a genuine factory-made outfit of female attire that has actually been incorporated into the design. This bear in question was such a bear, having limbs of red felt, covered with a green striped dress. Only the paws and head were of mohair. This particular bear had several things going for it. The obvious original female design, and an appearance that suggested a background that begged to be researched. It had two negatives that had to be carefully weighed. One was some damage done to the head when some well meaning human decided that this lady would look good with wire rim glasses, and had the nerve to poke the bows right through the face! I admit that our ear design doesn't always lend itself to a comfortable fit for eyeglasses, but to jab the wire right through the mohair is almost too painful to think about.

A second negative was the price. This is not to imply that we Teddies can be overvalued. Perish the thought! But on occasion some humans must consider the expenditure in relation to such mundane things as having enough left to eat, buy clothing, shelter and other such luxuries. After a few moments of mumbling, a couple of "what do you think?" comments, and a raised eyebrow or two, the Michauds agreed that this Teddy was worth acquiring if for no other reason than to remove those horrible glasses and perform reconstructive surgery on this poor lady.

Discovery time came at the first annual Teddy Tribune Convention in Minneapolis in 1983. The Michauds were sharing their collection with the audience and commented about the lady bear. After they finished, well-known author Pat Schoonmaker came up to tell Terry and Doris that this bear was actually one of a set of bears made as Mama, Papa and Baby Bear. She had seen the complete set at the Philadelphia Zoo Rally. This information not only enlightened the Michauds, but it added the challenge of finding the rest of the set.

Now our story takes place at a small shop in Mackinaw City, Michigan, where Terry and Doris were showing their collection at the Voyageur shop, owned by long-time friends the Crandalls. During the course of the day, a lady carrying a small paper bag appeared and stood quietly back as the Michauds entertained a small group of visitors. As they completed their conversation and the crowd dispersed, the lady stepped forward and inquired, "I wonder if you could tell me anything about this bear?" As Terry opened the bag and extracted an 11in (27.9cm) Teddy in red felt pants and blue jacket, he beamed and said, "I certainly can! This baby's mother has been looking for him for years!"

After filling in the details to the slightly startled lady, the question of purchase was brought up. She had no interest in selling the bear, but she was completely captivated by "Just Ted," a handcrafted creation Terry and Doris were just introducing. A trade was suggested, and both parties left that day feeling a little richer.

Alas, the third portion of this story is yet to be written, for somewhere out there Papa Bear is patiently waiting for a kind soul to return him for a family reunion at the Carrousel Museum. So, if you see Papa Bear, please ask him to call home.

OPPOSITE PAGE: *Mama is gold mohair with felt outfit and body. 13in (33cm). Baby is well worn brown mohair with same felt construction. 11in (27.9cm).*

Green With Envy

One of the regular doll shows attended by the Michauds is the Illinois Doll Show, held each summer in Peoria, sponsored by the Buckley family. Did I mention this show in a previous story about the Wizard of Oz Bears? Well, no matter, for if I haven't told that story yet, I will later. It's difficult to remember all these details when you're head is crowded with straw!

Terry and Doris have become friends with many of the regular dealers, including two ladies who specialize in wonderful dolls. The two dealers share a special relationship, being Mother and Daughter. Valda, the mother, comes from Michigan, while her daughter Fritzie lives in Illinois. They each operate their own antique doll business, but frequently are found at the same shows. Both dealers share another common bond, in that they both are especially fond of Teddy Bears. It is surprising, in fact, that they offer Teddies to the public from time to time. But they, too, have

probably learned the same lesson as the Michauds, that you can't have them all. One must occasionally part with a Teddy no matter how painful, in order to procure that next special bear.

While setting up for the 1982 Illinois Doll Show, Terry and Doris moved their merchandise in to the vicinity of their assigned tables, then covered it up so they could go treasure hunting. Stopping only long enough to exchange a "nice to see you again," our hunters moved rather quickly through the rows of tables, pausing only briefly to peer into the inner recesses of a partially opened packing box. As they approached Fritzie's booth, Doris spotted a magnificent 24in (61cm) Teddy with very long mohair pile. "Where on earth did you come up with this guy," Doris asked Fritzie, who had an armload of dolls she had just removed from their traveling container.

As is usually the case with most dealers, Fritzie was unable to pinpoint the origin. This is not

Teddy Bears were made in many colors and sizes.

uncommon, since many of these dealers buy collections and estates, and they buy from other dealers who can't always fill in the missing blanks.

Now it should be noted that everyone concerned (Doris, Terry, and Fritzie) were under the impression that this bear was the standard faded grey color. That is, until Doris happened to tip the head slightly, and peering into the crevice between the head and body, she exclaimed, "My God, he's green!"

Green he was, and even more green he is now, as Doris treated the bear to a careful bath in Murphy's Oil Soap. (Note, the Michauds have changed their cleaning methods twice since. They discovered Woolite did a nice job cleaning, and now their newest method came as a result of a sample of Formula Ten from Steve Gardner.)

Although this jolly green giant bears no labels, Terry and Doris are certain that he is of English ancestory, due to his British facial characteristics.

The story of the green bear took yet another interesting twist. As Doris exchanged funds, Terry cradled the big bear in his arms and started back to their booth. As he reached the vicinity of Valda's booth, the temptation to show off the latest find overcame him, and he hailed Valda with, "Look what we just found, a marvelous green Teddy Bear." "He's gorgeous," Valda said, "Where did you find him?" "I just purchased him from your daughter," Terry replied. "From Fritzie?! Wait til I see her. She knows I love Teddy Bears, and green is my favorite color!" was the response, filled with half shock and half mock anger.

This, of course, gave Terry the amunition he needed, as he made a point of passing Valda's booth frequently during the day, with quiet comments like, "Know where a guy can buy a green Teddy Bear?" and other assorted barbs. But then Terry never was good at letting sleeping dogs lie.

A delightful British Teddy from the early 1930s. 24in (61cm).

Tea Time

The Michauds are doing fewer and fewer antique shows these days, what with the fame of their handcrafted Teddy Bears spreading across the country. However, they are doing many more personal appearances with the Carrousel Museum Collection. Since I am the cornerstone bear in this famous collection, I am generally front and center in the touring display. Mind you, all of the Teddy Bears in this famous collection are not allowed to attend these shows, because there simply isn't room to take them all along. We must also take into consideration that some of my fellow bruins have to stay home and mind the museum, lest it be bare (pun intended).

Since I do get to attend all of the personal appearances, I am in a favored position to speak of them, and I must tell you that one of my personal favorites takes place every fall in Toledo, Ohio. A chain of stores known as Hobby Center Toys is headquartered there, and they annually sponsor a doll and Teddy Bear affair that has grown to be one of the largest in the country. Beth Savino and her family are the dynamic people who pull this whole thing together, and they fill an entire mall with who's who and what's what in the doll and Teddy Bear world.

The Carrousel Museum Collection has become part of this annual event, and every year Terry and Doris must decide which Teddies get to go. For weeks before the bears are chosen, most of them are on their best behavior. Unfortunately, there is some shoving and pushing by a very few at the last minute, but this kind of unbearlike behavior counts against those who participate.

Since our very beginning, Teddy Bears have been made in an almost endless variety of sizes, colors, shapes and styles, and certainly in about every fabric known to man. But it has always been a source of amazement to me the variation of non-bear items that were produced. First, let's define our terms. A non-bear item is any item that utilizes the popularity of the Teddy Bear image, but is not made in a plush material. For example, our likeness has been used on items of clothing, including hats, scarves, shirts and an endless variety of wearing apparel. Our classic shape was formed into silver baby rattles, teething rings, pins, and you name it.

8½ x 11in (21.6 x 27.9cm) tin tea tray with 3¼in (8.3cm) tea pot.

The Lithographer's art certainly has its share of cherished Teddy Bear creations. One of the most treasured items of this type came to the Michauds in 1983 while they were attending the big Teddy Bear event in Toledo, Ohio. These shows and appearances always bring out a number of Teddy Bears and their owners, and occasionally one is offered to Terry and Doris for their extensive collection.

It was during the 1983 Toledo show that the Michauds were approached by a lady in her sixties, who stopped by to ask Doris if she had any interest in Teddy Bear related toys. Doris assured her that they did, and the lady produced a small box that was opened to reveal a tissue-wrapped tin tray. This beautifully lithographed piece depicted five Teddies and two baby bears cavorting on it. It was accompanied by a 3in (7.6cm) high tin tea pot with lid, and showed the same bears at play.

The pleasant woman was somewhat apologetic because the complete set couldn't be found, but she explained that many years ago her family lost everything in a house fire, and the only possession of hers that was saved was part of the tea set. She had attended the show the previous year, and was so moved by the stories of some of the Teddy Bears in the collection that she wanted her tea set to be a part of this assemblage of childhood treasures. The years of dedication and effort that have gone into bringing together the Carrousel Museum Collection are more than compensated for by people such as the dear elderly woman who was willing to share some wonderful childhood memories.

Even American Teddy Bears enjoy tea time.

In Memory of Tommy

The never ending search for old Teddy Bears takes the Michauds on roads and byways not usually traveled by tourists. They find it not only scenic to pass through small towns and villages, but it also affords them the opportunity to stop at out-of-the-way antique shops where an occasional treasure can be found.

It was on such a secondary road in southern Michigan that Terry and Doris acquired a Teddy with a poignant past. They were returning from their tri-annual trip to one of their favorite toy shows, the St. Charles, Illinois, show that is sponsored by the publishers of *Antique Toy World* Magazine, and a show where a significant number of Teddy Bears in the Carrousel Collection have been acquired. This particular show had not produced its usual treasure, so Terry suggested they take a little extra time returning to Michigan and visit some shops on the way back. Since they had made the trip many times over the years, it was getting more and more difficult to take a new and different route, but a review of the road map showed a two lane road that wound its way through a number of small farming communities in the Southwestern section of the state. Since it was Monday, it was even more difficult to find an

antique shop open, but it was a pleasant sunny day, and a new route always added unique scenery.

As they rounded a curve and found themselves on the Main Street of yet another small community, Terry glanced left and Doris checked shops to the right as they slowly progressed through the three block business district.

"There's a shop" Terry commented, pulling the car to the curb quickly. As is typical of many antique shops in small communities, it offered the usual array of used furniture and bric-a-brac of a not too distant time. In the center of the shop a table was heavily laden with glassware and odds and ends taken from the cupboards of neighboring farm houses. A small wall shelf served as an anchor at one end of the table, and lying against it (or half sliding into the jumble of plates) was an 18in (45.7cm) Teddy whose grey and dusty appearance spoke of many years tucked away in someone's attic. Some kindly mother had outfitted this bear in a red cotton shirt and blue overalls, although time had taken its toll on the brightness of the colors. Even with his forelorn look, the Michauds felt this bear would be very comfortable in their collection, so an inquiry was made, the price was paid, and the Carrousel Collection grew by one.

A well loved 18in (45.7cm) Teddy comes out of the attic.

Shortly after arriving home, Doris removed the soiled clothing and put it in the laundry, where years of accumulated dust were washed away. Ironing the pants led to one of those marvelous little discoveries that add a special joy to collecting. As the iron glided over the pants pocket, a small lump appeared, and examining the contents of the pocket revealed that tucked away in the inner recesses was Teddy's very own monogrammed handkerchief!

Terry and Doris had developed a habit of inquiring about the background of Teddy Bears when they find them, but on this particular occasion they had neglected to raise any questions. Several months passed by, and on a visit to a fairgrounds antique show they chanced upon a booth operated by the owners of the antique shop where they had purchased the bear. This provided them with the opportunity to inquire about its origin. They were told that the Teddy Bear had belonged to a friend of the shop owner, and as luck would have it, their friend had accompanied them to the show. She pointed him out, sitting at a picnic table under a large shade tree. A pair of seersucker trousers were supported by faded red suspenders over a wool

plaid short buttoned at the neck. He was just as you might picture a gentleman of eighty plus years. Since the Teddy was of a 1920s vintage, it was not likely to be this man's Teddy.

The Michauds introduced themselves and inquired about the bear, and as the old man told the story, his eyes filled with tears. The bear, it seems, was purchased for his son Tommy in 1924, and the two of them were inseparable through his developing years. As with most childhood treasures, the bear was put away in the attic when Tommy became too old for a Teddy Bear.

Tommy graduated from High School in 1942, and went off to the Army to defend his country. Tommy was killed in battle on the beaches of Normandy.

A long pause ensued while the gentleman regained his composure. Then, he continued, "We sold the farm this past spring and moved into town to a smaller place. While cleaning out the attic we found the bear."

It seemed just too painful for him to continue. Doris assured him that the bear had an honored spot in their collection, and they left him to his memories.

Love remains forever.

A salute to you, Tommy, from an old friend.

An All Consuming Hunger

If you are beginning to get the impression that the entire Carrousel Museum Collection was acquired either in Britain or at the Chicago Toy Show, you are only partly correct. It is true that many of the special Teddy Bears in the collection were purchased in St. Charles, Illinois, at the Toy World show. That is due in great part to the fact that the Michauds have been doing this show three times a year almost since its inception, and many of the regular dealers have come to know them, and contact them when they turn up a Teddy treasure. But most of the time, Terry and Doris have to race through the show ahead of a horde of other arctophiles on the hunt.

When one is pressured by the fact that there are some five hundred tables of goodies to examine and precious little time to do it in, there is always a danger of missing a Teddy hiding behind a tin toy, or buried under a pile of dolls. A near miss occurred about eight years ago when Terry rounded a corner, glanced into the first booth in row four, spotted what appeared to be a bag bear, and stopped only because it had a rather strange looking mouth.

Let me explain that most bag bears (non-jointed bears) are of a more recent era, and therefore not as sought after by the bear collector who is attempting to build a collection that will mature in value.

Picking the bear up revealed that it was indeed a bag bear, but the unusual mouth opened wide when the head was tilted back to allow the owner to actually feed the Bear! This cinnamon Teddy was known as "The Feed Me Bear" and had a ravenous appetite for Animal Crackers. As purchased, he stood 15in (38.1cm) tall, and had missing eyes and only a few threads of his stitched nose remained. Pat Schoonmaker's authoritative book *The Collector's History of the Teddy Bear* gave much of the background information on this charming 1935 mechanical Teddy, showing a picture of a magazine ad of the bear wearing his "Feed Me" bib, which Doris has duplicated.

One might wonder how such a small Teddy Bear could consume mountains of Animal Crackers without bursting at the seams. A close examination reveals that a metal tube is connected to the mouth, and access is gained to the bottom of the tube by turning the bear over, unzipping his back, allowing removal of said Animal Crackers.

"Feed Me" bear nearly always gets to travel with the touring group, because he brings forth a volley of "Ooooohs" and "Ahhhs" from the crowd every time he is demonstrated.

LEFT: *Animal Crackers removed from back of Feed Me Bear, 1937, by Commonwealth Toy & Novelty Company.*

OPPOSITE PAGE: *15in (38.1cm) of all-consuming hunger.*

The Roosevelt Bears

One of the most frequently asked questions at the Carrousel Museum is "do you have an original Roosevelt Bear?" The inquiry is generally in reference to the first Teddy Bear, attributed to both Steiff and the founders of the Ideal Toy Corporation, the Mitchom family.

To my knowledge there was never a plush Teddy Bear produced that was specifically named The Roosevelt Bear. The confusion may be due in part to the great popularity of a series of children's books written by Seymour Eaton. This author of the early 1900s enthralled thousands of readers with the ongoing adventures of the Roosevelt Bears named Teddy B. and Teddy G. Each title gave the reader a clue as to that particular adventure, such as *The Traveling Bears in New York, The Traveling Bears in England, The Traveling Bears in Fairyland*, and a variety of other adventures. The books are in such great demand by collectors today that they are being reproduced. The Carrousel Museum Collection contains several copies of the original books, including one volume in its original dust jacket.

The Roosevelt Bears found their likeness else-where, including post cards, children's games and other printed matter, no doubt a move by the publisher to capitalize on their popularity. While the Michauds have focused their Teddy collecting on bears like myself of the plush species, they do occasionally enhance the accumulation with Teddy Bears represented on china, on lithographed tin, and in printed matter. A sterling example of a treasured non-plush Teddy item is a rubber stamp set with a beautiful lithographed cover picture showing Teddy B. and Teddy G. dancing as an organ grinder plays his music box. Inside the box are fifteen rubber stamps of various images, including dogs, rabbits, clowns, and, of course, bears. One stamp shows the Roosevelt Bears in an open touring car.

The Roosevelt Bears were represented in every media except plush, but recently D&D Productions in Baltimore, Maryland, designed Teddy B. and Teddy G. in plush form, and had them produced in England. They have managed to capture the charm and appeal of the early Roosevelt Bears, and the pair have been added to the Carrousel Museum Collection.

Contemporary Teddy B. and Teddy G. by D & D Promotions.

A Shaggy Dog Story

What is a dog story doing in a book about Teddy Bears you ask? Well I was a bit skeptical when Terry suggested I might want to include something about their miniature Schnauzer in this book, but I will have to say that a proportionately large number of arctophiles are also pet owners, and particularly dog lovers.

The Pet Connection can even lead to meeting fellow arctophiles. Take, for example, the time about eight years ago when the Michauds were "doing an antique market," as they would say. This was a rather large outdoor show that was held at a fairgrounds in a small community in northern Ohio. They had their tables set up under the shade of a tent awning, and were enjoying a warm sunny day with their dog Brodie at their side.

A couple approached, and the lady said "Oh, what a darling little Schnauzer. Can I hold him? We just lost ours a short time ago. My name is Peggy Bialosky and this is my husband Alan." Well, one thing led to another, and it was soon discovered that the two couples shared another common bond. This friendship has since grown, and the Michauds have watched as Peggy and Alan's books have contributed strongly to the growth of the present focus on Teddy Bears. Peter Bull is unquestionably the father of the movement, but the Bialoskys can be recognized as mid-wives (or mid-husbands) to today's mania.

Aw, gee! I was just playing with it.

Brodie (or Deacon Brodie of Edinburgh to be formal) hasn't been in the family nearly as long as I have. I wasn't the least bit jealous on his arrival, as I have known of the endless capacity for love demonstrated by arctophiles and/or dog owners. But I will have to confess that I, along with the other bears present at the time, had some concern for the sharpness of this dog's teeth. He could shred a cardboard box faster than you could fill it with doggie toys.

I am happy to report that Brodie has never once attacked me or any of the other Teddies in the Michaud household. As you can imagine, with such an extensive collection there are literally Teddy Bears everywhere. Once in a great while I have seen Brodie pick up a small bear from a window sill and take it over to Doris or Terry and drop it at their feet. His message, of course, is "pay a little attention to me guys, because I could make this bear into a pile of sawdust." A friendly scolding and a pat on the head seems to reassure him that he is still an important part of the family.

For those interested in the technical details, Brodie stands 14in (35.6cm) tall, has black shoe button eyes and is fully jointed. His hump on the back is not nearly as pronounced as mine, but there does seem to be indications of one.

Brodie is right at home with his friends.

When Irish Eyes Are Smiling

It is unfortunate that the bear makers of days gone by didn't make more of an effort to identify their product in some way. Steiff, of course, has their button in the ear, but beyond that the Teddy Bear craftsmen were negligent in this matter. It can be argued that no one at that time could have foreseen the demand by adult collectors for their product, for they were, after all, making playthings for children. There are scattered examples in the Carrousel Collection (and other collections one assumes) that have a foot label from Chad Valley in England, or a metal button on the chest by Grisley of Germany. But by and large, few of the older bears were labeled by their makers.

It's always a pleasant experience when an arctophile discovers his latest acquisition proudly carries the name of its producer. On a bear hunting expedition to Camden Passage in London, England, on their last trip, the Michauds discovered a small but delightful shop operated by Pam Heebs. This English lady has dealt in collectible dolls for a number of years, but found her shop being taken over more and more by Teddy Bears. Not much larger than a very large closet, this place is none the less crowded with bears of every vintage and appeal. The Michauds were so pleased with this shop that they returned several times during their brief stay.

Getting ready for St. Patrick's Day.

This was the original home of no less an important Bearoness than My Lady Camden, who's makers proudly emblazoned their name on a distinctive foot tag. I'm sure you can guess that the shelves of this shop had a great deal more room after the Michauds' visit.

The one and only Teddy Bear in the entire Carrousel Museum Collection that is known to have originated in Ireland came from this very shop. It was love at first sight when Terry spotted him sitting on the very topmost shelf. If you don't have enough horizontal room in your shop, you expand vertically, and it was obvious that Pam had added shelving that reached clear to the ceiling. Terry has a pretty good reach, particularly when it requires gathering in a Teddy Bear, but this lovable bear with a twinkle in his eye managed to stay out of reach until a three legged stool was used to give Terry the added reach needed. It was almost like there was a little Leprechaun inside saying "catch me if you can."

This 17in (43.2cm) Teddy has a unique head design that requires four pieces of mohair instead of the usual three. He has golden mohair with brown velvet pads, and the small label at the back of his neck says "Pedigree - Made in Ireland."

As Terry stepped off the stool with his Irish friend, he said "We'll take this Irish bear, but he wants his hat back" as he reached over and removed a green felt derby from a nearby doll. "Done" said Pam, and the two have been swapping old sea stories ever since.

Irish Bear is well identified on back of neck.

Me & My Shadow

The Carrousel Museum Collection is made up largely of Teddy Bears that have attained the age of forty years or more. This tendency toward the seasoned is due largely to the Michauds' love for the playthings of another era.

Occasionally a Teddy will join the family that has some other desirable characteristic, and it may or may not be known at the time of purchase. A visit to London's famous Portobello Road Flea Market in 1983 brought Doris face to face with a most unusual knitted bear. But before we tell you about this special Teddy, let's divulge a few bear hunting secrets developed over the years by the Michauds. First, if it's a well-known flea market, antique market or Teddy Bear Show, plan to arrive early. In fact, if you can be there early enough to help the dealers unpack, so much the better.

At one well-known London flea market you have to get there before dawn with flashlight in hand (or "torch," as they say in Britain) to get the best buys. You may still find a Teddy or two later in the morning, but it will likely have changed hands three or four times, with an accompanying inflation in price.

Secondly, plan to "skim shop" the first time around. That is, briskly go through the whole market or show and only stop at those places where you see a bear, or suspect there may be one. Now this will on occasion cause you to miss out on a fine bruin, but the odds are better if you get through quickly the first time around. If there are two of you, so much the better, as each can take a row or area with a prearranged signal to the other when a Teddy is spotted.

Thirdly, remain calm when the quarry comes in sight. Terry tends to quietly but firmly call out to Doris, but she more often than not lets out a shriek proportionate in volume to the appeal of the bear.

Now, about that special Teddy found at the Portobello Road Flea Market. You'll have to forgive my mental sidetrips, but it seems to go with the territory for those of us in our advanced years. Doris was making her way through a crowded section with Terry within earshot, when she spotted what appeared to be a knitted Teddy. The signal was given, and Terry quickly rushed to her side, casually inquiring about her find.

"I want to buy this knit bear, honey" Doris said, "He's kind of neat." "Save your money for fur" Terry admonished her. "We didn't come half way around the world for knit, we came for fur!" You must first recognize that Terry is prone to overstating the case to make a point, but in this case I would have supported his feelings.

Returning to his assigned area, it was but a minute or two before he was again called back by Doris. "Terry, I really want to buy this bear. Don't ask me why, but there's something special about him," she said. This time, Terry recognized that the tone of her voice was more of a statement than an appeal. Having long ago recognized the moment to retreat, Terry inquired "How much is it?" "Three Pounds," Doris responded. "Big deal! Five Dollars. So buy it," Terry said, breathing a sigh of relief having won on financial grounds if not on good taste.

Even though the outward appearance led Terry to believe the bear to be a handcrafted product of recent vintage, its classic shape appealed strongly to Doris, and she simply would not leave without him. An exchange of funds was made and the knit bear was packed into one of the special soft side bags purchased specifically for the purpose of transporting Teddy Bears. He and 35 or 40 of his peers made the trip back, some to join the collection, and some to be sold to fellow arctophiles.

A month or more passed by after their return, and the knit bear and his companions lay quietly on a large table awaiting further attention. Doris was visited one day by a friend, who was admiring the recent acquisitions. Doris thrust the knit bear at her friend, and said "Jan, you knit. Look how well this bear is made." "Gosh, he's really firm," Jan replied, "I wonder what he's stuffed with." The bear was returned to Doris' hands, who proceeded to give him a closer examination. "You know, it's almost as if there is something under the knitting," Doris responded, and no sooner had she spoken than she discovered a half hidden draw string tucked in the joint under the head. By now she was trembling, and she called out "Terry, come here!" as she untied the snug knot and loosened the knitting around the base of the head.

"Do you suppose ... there can't be ... there is!" Doris shrieked. "There's an old Teddy Bear under the knitting!" By now Terry, Doris and friend Jan were wide-eyed and giddy with delight as this marvelous 1920s Teddy made his first exposure to the light of day in many years. Each covering, separately made for each arm, leg, torso and head, was carefully removed and a Teddy Bear emerged that was so loved, he had been patched and re-patched until it seemed he no longer had room for another patch. So in order to give him added life, some kindly mother or grandmother had literally knitted a new covering for him! The new outer skin was made complete with button holes for the original eyes to come through, and glove-like ears for a comfortable fit over the original ears. The Michauds' Bear-making skills were put to use to join and stuff the outer shell so that it could be recreated as it was found. Needless to say, Terry is not quite so quick to pass by what seems to be a nondescript Teddy Bear.

I would hope and pray that this story does not cause a stampede of arctophiles to return home and randomly prod, poke and otherwise abuse a Teddy in hopes of finding an older Teddy lurking under a false skin. But one can't help but wonder just how many velveteen Teddy Bears there are out there, waiting to be discovered.

Knitted Bear and the well loved Teddy found inside!

The Duke of Portobello

Terry and Doris made their first trip to Britain in celebration of their 25th Anniversary in 1975. There have been three subsequent trips in 1977, 1980 and 1983. With the present favorable exchange rate, it's a wonder they haven't made yet another trip.

At any rate, many of my brothers can be traced to England. It is my understanding that the selection there has dimmed, and prices have caught up with prices here in the United States, but that should not daunt you from making a bear excursion to Britain, or anywhere for that matter. The cardinal rule for bear hunting remains "expect a Teddy to turn up in the most unexpected place."

One of the favorite hunting grounds in England for arctophiles and antique collectors alike is the world famous Portobello Road Flea Market, an event held every Saturday in London that seems to draw half the population of London as well as hordes of tourists. This colorful market runs for several blocks, with dealers lining both sidewalks, and row after row of buildings crammed with vendor's stalls.

During their 1980 visit, the Michauds made the Saturday pilgrimage to the Portobello Market with the usual high level of anticipation. Mid-morning found them about half way through the maze of old and not so old merchandise. Doris and daughter

The Duke of Portobello has discovered one of Terry's antique toys.

Kim entered a door leading into one of the indoor market areas, while Terry entered the same area from the far side of the building.

Moments after entering, Doris spotted The Duke of Portobello (so named in honor of his place of discovery) and reached out to gather him from the dealers shelf as she excitedly turned to Kim and said "Go and get your father!" Terry arrived in time to see Doris putting her wallet back into her purse, with The Duke cradled tightly under her left arm.

The only blemish on this otherwise magnificent English Teddy was an orange crayon stain on the tips of a small patch of mohair on his chest, which was subsequently corrected by delicate surgery with manicure scissors. The Duke is oversize as the average Teddy goes, standing 28in (71.1cm) from his flat soled feet to the top of his head. He is believed to be of English origin, which brings up a subject I should address here and now.

It is worth noting that most of the Teddies purchased in England on this and other trips were Bears of English ancestry, a fact that seemed to surprise Terry, who had somehow anticipated discovering a large number of German Teddy Bears. Had he asked me, I would have suggested he go to Germany to find German Teddies, but then I am not always consulted on such matters.

During a visit the next day with the late Peter Bull, he inquired if they had been able to find any nice Teddy Bears during their trip. Doris described her discovery of the Duke of Portobello at the antique market the previous day. Peter asked if he might see this magnificent Bear, and when told it had been packed up in a box and shipped back, a smile crossed his lips as he exclaimed "Well! He certainly won't like that, you know!"

Chapter Two of the Duke's story took place back in the United States, or "the Colonies" as a Briton might say. While attending a doll show in Detroit, Michigan, Terry spotted a wool sailor suit, and picking it up for a closer look, he commented "looks like it might fit the Duke." Checking the label inside, the Michauds were amazed and delighted to discover that this garment had been made in London, England! The Duke appeared in his sailor suit in one of the famous Bialosky calendars, and he has since acquired a genuine British sailor hat to compliment his outfit.

The Duke of Portobello, as found in London. 28in (71.1cm)

Doris with her favorite Bear.

My Lady Camden

The Duke of Portobello made a reasonably comfortable adjustment to his new life in the Carrousel Collection, but after a time he began to show signs of being homesick. It wasn't all that obvious at first, but I became suspicious when he started demanding tea every afternoon at four o'clock. This type of behavior is not at all typical of the Duke. His entire attitude changed for the better when Doris and Terry returned from their last trip to Britain and introduced the Duke to My Lady Camden, who has been his constant companion since their first meeting. It's even difficult to get him away long enough to discuss British politics and other important matters.

My Lady Camden is of fine English aristocracy and has a label to confirm it, although she has such fine bearing (no pun intended) and presence that it is obvious to even the most untrained eye. She is a 23in (58.4cm) Teddy in a beautiful pale gold long mohair. The label on her right foot reads as follows: "By Appointment to//H.M. Queen Elizabeth//the Queen Mother//Toymaker//The Chad Valley Co. Ltd."

My Lady Camden, 1930s English Teddy. 23in (58.4cm).

Before her introduction to her peers, My Lady Camden was appropriately outfitted in a simple but elegant lace collar held in place with a beautiful English cameo brooch. Many years ago Doris had put away one of those very special items that had a destiny that was not known at the time, but became obvious when the Michauds met My Lady Camden. It is a lovely tiara that was once worn by Doris' mother for special dress up occasions in the 1930s.

My Lady Camden feels so elegant with it that she has not removed it since the day it was placed on her head.

Although most ladies are reluctant to discuss their age, I can tell you that My Lady Camden is young, indeed, with an estimated origin in the late 1940s or early 1950s. She is much younger than the Duke, but I must admit they do make a lovely couple.

Two good friends catch up on the news from home.

Somewhere Over The Rainbow

We promised earlier to tell you about the Wizard of Oz bears, and there is no time like the present. In making preparations for their regular trek to the Illinois Doll Show in Peoria, some thought had to be given to the theme of the show, which changed every year. For the 1978 theme, the Buckley family had chosen The Wizard of Oz as the central focus. This meant that doll dealers would be scrambling to come up with various and sundry ways of showing Dorothy and the other Oz characters.

Since Terry and Doris always try to build their theme around their antique bears, it seemed only natural to come up with Teddy Bears appropriately dressed as the central characters. For Dorothy, a wool plush bear of English origin from the 1940s was chosen. She had a dress that seemed appropriate, so Doris simply had to add the red felt shoes. Dorothy stands 14in (35.6cm) tall. In the wicker basket on her arm the Michauds placed a chocolate colored miniature jointed Schuco Teddy from the 1970s. He relished his role at Toto Bear.

Next a 16in (40.6cm) English mohair Teddy Bear was chosen for the role of Cowardly Bear. A mane and tail of dark gold plush were all that was needed for his attire. Scare Bear, the largest of the group, is a 17in (43.2cm) rayon plush Teddy from the 1930s, and his cinnamon plush with gold insert nose contrasts nicely with his straw suit, held in place by his red and white checked overalls. Tin Bear is also from the 1930s.

Although Dorothy Bear is considered the central character in this cast, there is one role that the Teddy Bears nearly all wanted. I must confess that even I had fancied the role, as I knew it would be great fun to play. That was the role of Witchie Bear, and the honor went to an older Teddy than the rest of the cast. A 13in (33cm) jointed mohair Teddy with sparkling shoe button eyes won the assignment, and he certainly seems well suited to the part. He got decked out in an appropriate black cape and typical witch's hat. But the "piece d'occasion" (piece for a special occasion, for those of you not fluent in French) was the nose. Everyone is well aware that a witch has a nose of peculiar shape totally unlike that of a Teddy Bear nose. I can't say for certain where Witchie Bear rounded up the black leather for her nose, but I recall hearing Terry bellow "Who cut the tongue out of my black dress shoes?"

Our cast of characters were appropriately set up in front of a backdrop of a forest, with a castle shown in the distance. It apparently impressed the judges, because our bears returned home not only with a trophy for First Place, but a ribbon and trophy for Best of Show as well. You can imagine how envious all the dolls at the show were, and I can tell you that our Teddy Bears were so proud that they have remained in their costumes ever since.

LEFT: Dorothy's friends include Cowardly Bear, an English mohair Teddy, 16in (40.6cm). Tin Bear, a 14½in (36.9cm) cinnamon mohair Bear; and Scare Bear, a wool two-tone plush Teddy, c.1935, 17in (43.2cm).

OPPOSITE PAGE: Dorothy is wool plush with jointed arms, nonjointed head and legs. 14in (35.6cm). Toto is a mohair Schuco, 3½in (8.9cm). Witchie is 1920s Teddy. 13in (33cm).

Teddy's Two Cousins

Steiff Koala enjoys climbing. 4½in (11.5cm).

The truth has to come out sooner or later, and I guess it is just as well that it comes from a fellow bear, so I suppose it is proper that I reveal this long kept secret. The fact of the matter is, there are two Teddy Bears amongst us who are not, technically speaking, Teddy Bears. However, they are not aware of this, and so they enjoy a most happy welcome in collections everywhere.

I am referring of course, to the Panda and the Koala. Now before I am inundated with irate letters from arctophiles (or from Pandas and Koalas, for that matter) let me implore you to take a little time to study an Encyclopedia (or a National Geographic) and get the factual background on the two bears in question. I cannot in good conscience take the time and trouble in this book to detail the life history of either species, but fact is fact, and the fact is, the Panda and the Koala are not Teddy Bears. If a world wide conference was held today by arctophiles, I am certain that a motion could be entertained and unanimously passed to adopt both creations as full fledged members. I cannot imagine a collection of Teddy Bears without a representative Panda and/or Koala.

That feeling is certainly shared by the Michauds, who have several of each in this collection. Two that were recently acquired at Linda Mullins show in San Diego, California, are a Steiff Koala and a Hermann Panda. The Koala has a jointed head, large felt nose, paws and feet, with a beautiful beige mohair body. He was made in the 1950s. The Panda is fully jointed and is unusual in that he does not have black eye patches. His plush is rayon, which would indicate that he is of Post World War Two vintage.

One of Doris' fondest memories of England was a visit to the Zoo in London to see their real live Panda. You can be sure that both Pandas and Koalas will always be welcome in the Carrousel Museum Collection. When the appropriate time comes, the Michauds may tell their two charges that they are adopted, but that does not mean they are less loved; indeed, it means they are very special.

OPPOSITE PAGE: *Steiff Koala is joined by Hermann Panda. 7in (17.8cm).*

The famous profile of a mystery writer?

Alfred

Get a group of pet owners together and you can almost pick out which person owns which breed of dog. Attend a dog show and watch the owners parade their pets around the ring. More often than not the animal has many of the same physical characteristics of his master. One can't be certain if fate draws them together, or if the dog assumes some of the characteristics after having spent years practicing.

At any rate, I have come to the conclusion after years of study on the subject, that this same phenomenon can be found in arctophile circles. Ask a Teddy Bear person to produce a picture of his or her first bear, or better yet, to produce the actual bear. Study them closely. Notice how the drooping jowls of the master are reflected in the sagging mohair on the bear's face? Look at the bags under the eyes of the human and see the similarity to the deep set dark circles around the shoe button eyes on the bear. It would indeed be hasty to jump to the conclusion that this occurrence was more common than not. But it happens all too often to be totally ignored. Take, for example, Alfred.

Alfred came to the Michaud household perhaps a dozen years ago. He is a 1920s cinnamon mohair Teddy of English aristocracy. Poor Alfred was in a sad state of affairs on his arrival, with limbs falling loose and about to come off.

Surgery was in order considering his physical state, and the stitch ripper (comparable to a scalpel) was employed to carefully open him up. One hesitates to perform unneeded surgery, but when it is necessary, the bonus may be the discovery of something inside that helps to date the bear. This was the case with Alfred. It was learned that he was held together with wooden thread spools that had been cut in half to make his discs. The ends of the spools still had the label of the manufacturer, and it was typical of thread spools of the 1920s.

It wasn't until the surgery was completed and Terry was taking Alfred back to his resting place on the shelf when he caught a glimpse of his profile. "Alfred!" he shouted, turning him so the profile faced Doris. "Alfred Hitchcock!" they exclaimed in unison. Did this bear actually belong to the late and great movie director? The odds are against it, but I must tell you that it may be just a coincidence, but Alfred seems to spend much of his time reading mystery novels.

ABOVE: *Alfred's favorite past time.*

LEFT: *An Alfred Hitchcock look-a-like in cinnamon mohair. English origin. 16in (40.6cm).*

67

Bearkin

When an arctophile acquires a Teddy Bear, it is not always easy to know if the bear is entirely original as found, or if some loving grandmother has performed some sort of surgery on him. Granted, sometimes the stitching has been applied with a large measure of love and just a small measure of talent, but in some cases it is difficult to know.

Doris puzzled for some time over a small 8in (20.3cm) bear she acquired in 1981. It was certainly well made, and had many of the characteristics of a Steiff, but his most puzzling charactertistic was a red mouth and tongue. It was stitched in place, as you might expect in a bear of the 1930s era, but the color was not at all typical of anything the Michauds had encountered before.

There was a temptation to write it off as something some mother had added through the years, and to pull it out and replace it with an appropriate brown stitching to match the nose and claws. But as a rule, the Michauds like to keep the Teddies in their "as found" condition, unless the repair is needed to keep the bear from further damage. My ear surgery is a good case in point. True, I could hear out of my one ear, but when I reached the stage in life where I needed spectacles, it would have been rather difficult to hold them in place with only one ear.

At any rate, Pat Schoonmaker's book *The Collector's History of the Teddy Bear,* produced the answer, for on page 49 you'll find "Bearkin," a Teddy produced by Steiff for F.A.O. Schwarz in 1935. This charming fellow came complete with a trunk and wardrobe. He has clear glass eyes with black pupils, brown stitched nose and claws, and lo and behold, he has a red mouth! There are undoubtedly a number of collections out there that have Bearkin in his complete original state, but even this bare bear is most welcome in the Carrousel Museum Collection.

OPPOSITE PAGE: Bearkin in white mohair with red lips. 8in (20.3cm).

BELOW: Bearkin checks his wardrobe for a day's outing.

The Mysterious Lady of Connecticut

Early in their toy and doll collecting career, long before I came along to alter the Michauds' lives forever, they were eager to learn about all kinds of antiques. They were involved in those early days in the Midland Antique Society, a study group of other questers of varying interests in the antiques field. A number of friendship bonds were forged, and some of these people have been instrumental in helping to widen the scope of the Carrousel Museum Collection.

A sparkling personality from that early group named Rae Cooker dealt in a variety of items for collectors, and she particularly enjoyed finding unique Teddy Bears for the Michauds. One day during a visit to her shop Doris and Terry were presented with a sad looking 10in (25.4cm) Teddy Bear with a torn nose and not a shred of mohair left on his body. "I know he's not much," Rae said, "but I just didn't have the heart to throw him out. He belonged to my friend in Connecticut who has a number of Teddy Bears, and every now and then she is willing to part with one."

"Oh, he's got great character," Doris stated, "I can do a nosectomy on him, and look here! He's managed to hang on to his dignity. He's still got his original Steiff button!"

Moths and Silverfish have a yearning for mohair, which was likely the fate of this bear, but the pewter Steiff button would be a bit too much for even the hungriest of moths. The bear came home with the Michauds, and subsequent study has led to the discovery that this Teddy, like the puzzled bear's companion, is also an original of the Margaret Strong Edition by Steiff.

The bald Steiff from 1904 guards his friend, a white mohair Steiff, which is actually a baby rattle. Bald Steiff 10in (25.4cm). Baby Rattle 5½in (14cm).

The story of the lady in Connecticut was further enhanced by Rae, who went on to tell of a Teddy Bear that has traveled all over the world with this lady. "He has his own wardrobe that goes with him, and he goes wherever she goes," Rae said. "She's going to have to give some thought about what will become of that bear when she passes on, so if you don't mind, I'll let her know about you folks and your collection."

This event took place about five years ago. Just last year the Michauds were delightfully surprised to discover that the shop had acquired another bear from the Connecticut lady. This bear is a very small white mohair Steiff in excellent condition, and most remarkably it contains a baby rattle inside the plush torso. I must admit that even with my broad acquaintance and knowledge, I have never met a fellow bear quite like this one.

While these two Teddy Bears from Connecticut represent opposite ends of the scale as far as cash value is concerned, both Teddies share an equally large welcome at the Michaud residence. Perhaps some day, when the Carrousel Traveling Museum Collection pays a visit to Connecticut, the two bears will get to see their world traveling brother.

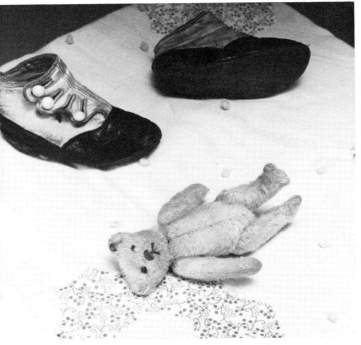

Steiff Baby Rattle spends nap time in the nursery.

With nearly every shred of mohair stripped away and a well patched head, our bald friend has retained his original Steiff button.

A Beauty From Bay City

Most of the personal appearances by the Michauds bring forth Teddy Bears of all ages and their happy owners with warm stories of their childhood. But on some occasions it is an emotional scene that more often than not produces tears. Such a meeting took place in Bay City, Michigan, in 1977, when Terry and Doris shared their collection with the public at a Teddy Bear affair. It had been announced in the local newspaper, and some interesting bears and bear owners showed up.

One delightful gentleman who is a captain on a Great Lakes freighter brought in his Teddy to visit, accompanied by Teddy's very own roadster. His bear was decked out in a knitted scarf and cap, as it was a chilly autumn day. The captain shared some wonderful stories of his childhood, starting with the discovery of the bear lying in a mud puddle. It was dried out and given a few needed repairs by a loving mother, and became a constant companion throughout his childhood. It was obvious that his attachment remained strong to the present day.

A friend can be so comforting.

Later in the afternoon Doris was approached by a lady carrying a brown grocery bag. With trembling face, she asked "Do you buy Teddy Bears?" "Yes, we do," Doris replied. "I mean, do you actually pay money for them?" the lady persisted. "Yes, we certainly do," Doris assured her. With that, the lady handed over the bag, and Doris removed an English Teddy measuring 21in (53.3cm), dressed in slip, baby dress, socks and crocheted booties.

"What a darling Bear!" Doris exclaimed. The lady's eyes were moist by now, and with trembling voice she explained "My father gave me this Teddy Bear in 1920. I dressed him in my own baby clothing, and I crocheted the booties for him when I first learned to crochet as a child."

"We would certainly be interested in buying your Teddy for our Collection" Doris responded. "How much do you want for him?" "Oh, I couldn't take any money. I just want you to have him," the woman said. "I knew that if you really pay money for Teddy Bears, you must really love them, and when I read about you in the paper, I knew my Bear would be in Teddy Bear Heaven." With that, the lady turned and walked away, and her sobbing could be heard as she disappeared down a hallway. Terry and Doris had moist eyes as well, and I seemed to have acquired a lump in my throat. Probably just shifting straw.

1920 English Teddy with new-found friends. 21in (53.3cm).

A Steiff Is Not A Steiff When It Is A Hermann

Terry is faced with a touchy dilemma when appraising or identifying Teddy Bears for people. It seems that everyone wants a winner, and many collectors want to believe that their bear is a Steiff. It is obviously a simple matter if the button is intact, but since many a worried parent removed the button, a fair number of Steiff animals have spent their days without that critical identifying mark. Terry is too much of a gentleman to tell the owner that in his opinion, their bear is not a Steiff. I think it may also have something to do with the fact that he is afraid of being pummeled on the spot with an oversize purse. I feel somewhat safe in discussing the matter, for who could think of beating up a defenseless old Teddy Bear?

The assumption by collectors that Steiff represents one of the finest works of craftsmanship is an accurate one. But one must also recognize that many other makers rank equally high. Teddy Bears made by Hermann in Germany share the same degree of top craftsmanship. Many of the English bears were and are remarkably well done. A Carrousel bear reflects a great deal of tender, loving construction. (I felt somewhat obligated to get that in, what with all of the kindnesses shown to me by the Michauds.)

Hermann open-mouth Teddy from 1954. 11in (27.9cm).

One of Terry's constant battles on the home front is in the arena of identifying bears. Doris (who is more often right than not, I must admit) is quick to pronounce "It's a Hermann" or "It's a Chad" or one of a host of other makers. Terry is just as quick to challenge her.

In more recent years Doris has gained an ally in Jane Servinski, the proprietress of Maple Hill Nursery and Doll Shoppe. Their acquaintance began as a desire by the Servinskis to handle the Carrousel line, but their friendship has since grown well beyond the boundaries of business.

Terry now has to do battle with both females, for when one proclaims "It's a Hermann," the other swears to it. At times I wish I could take sides, but I've found it's best to stay out of these things. Terry was certain he had them both dead to rights when a 1950s bear showed up a few years ago. It had an open mouth with air brushed features and Terry knew instantly that this was the popular Zotty by Steiff. Jane said "I think it's a Hermann," and Doris said "You're right, Jane, it is." "A Hermann!" snorted Terry. "You two wouldn't know a Hermann if it bit you!"

It was hardly an appropriate remark, since Hermanns are well-known for their gentleness, but his point was made none the less. "We're doing the Toledo Doll and Bear show next month, and both Mr. Steiff and Mr. Hermann will be there, so we'll see," said Doris. Terry and Doris were introduced at the show to Mr. Hermann by their friend Peter Kalinke, and the bear in question was handed over for examination. Mr. Hermann looked him over carefully and conversed in German with Peter. "What's wrong," Doris asked. Isn't it a Hermann?" "My dear, that is not in question, but Mr. Hermann is trying to remember which month in 1954 the bear was made!" Doris had decided to keep Terry around, since he is quite good at stuffing bears.

Left: Steiff Cosy. Center: Hermann open mouth. Right: Steiff Zotty from the 1950s.

An Unhappy Marriage

The year was 1908, and the popularity of the Teddy Bear was reaching epidemic proporitions (notice I said, 1908, not 1980). Doll makers everywhere huddled in small groups, pondering the fate of their creations during the upcoming Christmas season. Would little girls turn away from their traditonal playthings in favor of a fuzzy creation with a warm, engaging smile, and so huggable that even grownups couldn't resist him?

Alas, what to do in the face of such a dilemma! "I've got it!" shouted one manufacturer. "I'll have the best of both worlds, for this Christmas I will introduce the captivating Teddy Girl, with the body of the Teddy Bear, and the charm and appeal of a Doll face." The Teddy Girl was launched with great fanfare, and it was greeted with yawns and ignored by the buying public everywhere. The poor Teddy Girl enjoyed a very short life span, as she was withdrawn from the market place nearly as quickly as she was introduced.

It must be said that probably the greatest reason for the rejection of this strange creation is that it was uglier than sin, failing to capture the warmth and charm of a Teddy Bear. We can say that, due to

its unique place in history and relative rare status, it is highly desired by collectors. Terry and Doris count themselves fortunate indeed to have two of the typical Teddy Girls with celluloid faces in their collection, and one very rare Teddy Girl with a Simon & Halbig bisque head. We are not able to share a photograph of the rare bisque head Teddy Girl, as she is presently awaiting surgery in a Doll Hospital. It seems her bad luck story didn't end with her withdrawl from the market place. Doris was showing her off one day and she slipped from her hands and went crashing to the floor. Now a Teddy Bear would recieve a small bruise perhaps, or maybe a little straw shifting, but the poor Teddy Girl was much too fragile for such a tumble, and her head shattered into hundreds of pieces. Due to her rarity the Michauds will restore her, but she simply is in no condition to receive visitors at the moment.

LEFT: Grey mohair Teddy Girl 9½in (24.2cm). Gold Mohair Teddy Girl, 8½in (21.6cm).

RIGHT: Teddy Girls created by doll maker to recapture market lost to Teddy Bears.

Proxy

A public appearance by the Michauds, or a visit to the Carrousel Museum, has probably inspired hundreds of people to go home to rummage through their attics to find their very own Teddy Bear. It's always fun to have them stop back to share their bear. More often than not, they describe the bear as being "at least 18in (45.7cm) big," and after resurrecting him from the recesses of a trunk, they discover that the 18in (45.7cm) bear has shrunk to a wee little bear half the size they remembered him to be. Some great sage once said "It's only the eyes you are looking through," and that would certainly be appropriate in this case, for as the child records information in his memory banks, he sees an entirely different world than the adults around him. It is probably this childhood nostalgia that sparks many a beginning arctophile, whether they had a Teddy Bear as a child or not.

In the case of the Michauds, Terry was the youngest in a family of eight children, and although there are family photos showing the older brothers and sisters with a family bear, it never survived down to Terry. He accuses his family of hiding it away to this day. He is quick to tell people that if they didn't have a Teddy Bear as a child, they had a deprived childhood. Although one can say with certainty that he has more than made up for it!

Doris's childhood did indeed revolve around a Teddy Bear. Her family pictures show her at several stages of her young life, clutching her Teddy. Doris was the oldest in a family of two girls, and their mother taught them early in life the virtue of sharing their toys with those who were less fortunate. Less fortunate would be relative to where one was on the scale, and certainly the Martins had a sparse existence through the depression years. But they managed to get along due to the efforts of their hard working and loving parents.

When Doris recalls an early memory, she can see herself seated at her mother's dressing table, her jewel box open with several strands of costume jewelry draped over her bear's head. "He had rather large ears," she recalls, "and I believe he was made of that funny horsehair-type material that they made couches out of. I think my Dad had a pair of bedroom slippers made from the same kind of material."

Sadly we must say that this very bear did not accompany Doris on her path through life. It probably went to the little girl down the street who's father was out of a job. At any rate, Doris was fortnate to discover his proxy at a toy show in California about eight years ago. He stands 12in (30.5cm) high, has shoe button eyes and large ears, and is made of the same wool material she remembers as a child. No, he won't replace her childhood bear, but he serves as a reminder of a pleasant day gone by.

Doris with her Bear at age 3.

Doris with her bear at age 6.

The Dowager Twins

Twin Bears you say? It is rare, if not almost unheard of, to find two Teddies that are identical in every respect, even if made by the same person. Someone once asked Terry if he would sell any of his duplicate Teddy Bears. He said he probably would, but that he had never come across a duplicate Teddy yet.

However, this is not the story of Twin Teddies, but rather of twin ladies and their Teddy Bears. Doris and Terry have participated in doll shows long before there was such a thing as a Teddy Bear show. In fact, in those days Teddy Bears were usually relegated to a cardboard box under the dealer's table, if they were taken to a show at all.

One of the more popular doll events takes place several times a year in Lansing, Michigan. It is the same show, in fact, where I was discovered. Jean Canaday's shows are widely attended, and more than one Teddy Bear has found its way into the Carrousel Museum Collection by way of her doll show.

In 1975, while attending this popular show, one of the dealers produced two Teddies that shared similiar characteristics, including their 10in (25.4cm) size, and shoe button eyes. They differed in that one was originally white mohair with brown stitched nose and claws, while the other had its beginning as a brown mohair Teddy with black stitching. The dealer had acquired the Teddies from twin spinsters. It's always remarkable to find an original owner who is willing to part with their Teddy Bear, but can you imagine twins parting with theirs? Both Teddies show equal amounts of mohair being loved away, to the degree that Doris felt compelled to crochet matching sweaters for them.

Since the two Teddies were not received from the original owners, the Michauds were not able to learn their given names. They have since selected appropriate names, and these two charming Teddy Bears are now known as Donna and Dotty, the Dowager Twins. Any similarity in name to two ladies who operate a Teddy Bear emporium in Baltimore, Maryland, is purely intentional.

The Amos n' Andy Show entertains our spinster twins. **Left:** Brown mohair. **Right:** White mohair. 11in (27.9cm).

The Twins are easy to spot, even in a crowd of friends.

Yes/No In Small, Medium and Large

We have mentioned the German firm of Schuco several times. This company was probably better known as a maker of top quality metal cars and trucks for children, but they also produced a variety of mechanical Teddy Bears, most of which were activated by a key-wound spring.

One of the Schuco mechanical Teddy Bears that are in great demand by collectors are the Schuco Yes-No Bears. These Teddy Bears had the ability of nodding their heads yes or no, depending on the question put to them and the movement of their tail by the person holding the bear. The Yes-No bear came in several sizes and varieties, and the Carrousel Collection contains three widely differing examples.

First, there is the small Yes-No Teddy, 8½in (21.6cm) in size, and dressed in black checked trousers topped with a green felt jacket. The outfit is original, as one can see a muslin body under the clothing, a design made no doubt to save on mohair. This Schuco dates to the 1950s.

Next we have a very colorful Schuco Yes-No bear, who wears the black trousers, red jacket and cap of a bellhop uniform. This outfit is also original, as the felt uniform is actually part of the body. The bellhop stands 15in (38.1cm) tall, and is the oldest of this group, dating to the early 1930s.

Our last Schuco is by far the largest of the group, standing a full 21in (53.3cm) on his flat feet. He is made in a light grey mohair, and is believed to be from the late 1940s. This is substantiated by a book in the Carrousel Museum Collection that is titled "Edith the Lonely Doll," a picture book for children published in the 1950s. Edith's constant companion throughout the book is the Schuco Yes-No Teddy Bear.

I'm not the first Bear to be featured in a book, but I'll wager I'm one of the only Teddies to have written a book!

BELOW: *When the Schuco Yes/No Bears get together, heads really turn!*

Largest Yes/No Schuco in brown mohair. 21in (53.3cm).

Smallest Yes/No Schuco in original outfit.
8½in (21.6cm).

Oldest (and rarest) Yes/No in original Bell Hop
outfit.

Flo's Friend

A number of my fellow bears in the Carrousel Collection can claim to be involved in show business to one degree or another. Certainly the mechanical windups take center stage when it's time to entertain a crowd. An English Teddy with a delightful swiss music box can be called upon to amuse listeners. A very large group could be assembled to participate in a costume party at any given moment.

But when it comes to name dropping and a link to real fame, we'll have to take a bow to Eddie. This trouper goes all the way back to 1904, when he was given to Eddie Paige in Findlay, Ohio, by Marilyn Miller, who spent her summers with her family in Findlay, and did the vaudeville circuit under the name of the Five Columbians. Marilyn went on to greater fame and fortune in the Ziegfield Follies.

Eddie was brought to the Michauds in Louisville, Kentucky, where they were on tour at J. Cort Toys. He had been passed on to Eddie's brother Jimmy, then to sister Alice. Eddie is technically referred to as a Cone Head, but personally I would prefer some other descriptive title. He is 16in (40.6cm) tall, and has a rich cinnamon mohair that is most unusual. He has black shoe button eyes, and his long forearms make it easy for him to reach his toes. Although Eddie showed his age with several tears on his body, his felt pads were in mint condition, rare indeed for a Teddy of 81 years.

Needless to say, the Carrousel Bears are all ears when Eddie relates stories of Flo Ziegfield and early days of vaudeville.

LEFT: *Eddie is a cone head design in gold mohair, 1904, 16in (40.6cm).*

OPPOSITE PAGE: *There's no business like show business!*

South of The Border

This story doesn't start out South of the Border, but give me a little time and we'll get there. It actually starts farther north in the rather chilly climate of Minneapolis, Minnesota.

The year was 1982, and the Michauds were doing a personal appearance at a Teddy Bear rally in the twin cities. During the course of the day, a charming lady in her middle eighties came in carrying a Teddy Bear that caused those present to gasp with pure excitement. It was an early 20in (50.8cm) Steiff Teddy who wore his original leather muzzle. Terry pointed out to the lady that this bear was quite valuable, and to avoid damage to the Bear he suggested that she place it under a glass dome so that it could be shared, but protected. At the end of the day's events, the lady and her muzzled Teddy went on their way.

The following year the first Annual Teddy Tribune Convention was held in Minneapolis, and Teddy Bear fever was reaching new heights, evidenced by the huge crowds who waited patiently to enter the showrooms. They were well behaved (as you would expect of Teddy Bear people) in spite of the difficulty in working one's way around the room to view the hundreds of Teddies waiting to go to new homes.

Terry glanced up as a woman entered the booth, and immediately exclaimed, "How nice to see you again. I'm sorry I don't remember your name, but we met you last year when you brought in a most charming muzzled Teddy Bear. How is he, by the way?"

"Why, he's just fine," responded the lady, "but I've decided to sell him" "What a coincidence!" replied Terry, "because we've decided to buy him!"

A brief discussion followed, and an appointment was made for the following day to pay a visit to her home. It was obvious to Terry and Doris that this Teddy Bear was special, but he became even more valued when his history was related.

The Bear's owner stated that Teddy was given to her by her father in 1907, who had purchased him from the Butler Brothers Company in Minneapolis. There are many historical references to this company as one of the major distributors of toys and Teddy Bears in the United States just after the turn of the century. As the charming lady unfolded her story, it sparked a memory of yet an earlier Teddy! A short rummaging through a closet produced the Steiff Teddy Bear that is probably the earliest Teddy in the Carrousel Collection. She said that this bear had been given to her at birth in 1903. It was in need of repair to an arm and leg, and much of the original mohair had been loved away, but the muzzled Teddy and his older brother are now inseparable. The 1903 Teddy is the original of the bear that Steiff reissued in 1984 honoring the Margaret Strong Museum.

We promised in the beginning that we would take you South of the Border, and so we shall. Additional delightful information from the lady revealed that she owned a restaurant in Mexico City, and the muzzled Teddy Bear spent over forty years there! Imagine! All that spicy food and no way to enjoy it.

The Michauds still correspond with their friend, who continues to run the restaurant to this very day. She has a computer installed in her apartment, and has daily reports from South of the Border! No wonder she stays so young.

1907 rare Steiff muzzled Bear. 20in (50.8cm).

A rare pair enjoy their visit South of the Border.

Original 1903 Steiff and his recreated Steiff counterpart.

Christopher Robin's Friend

What would a Teddy Bear collection be without a Winnie the Pooh? Few children of today would recognize the Winnie of their grandparents' day, but in one form or another, he has delighted little ones and grownups alike through the years in the inspiring stories of A.A. Milne. Today, the largest distribution of modern day Winnies is through the world famous Sears, Roebuck and Company.

Doris was destined to be a Teddy Bear artist, for one of her projects in 1968 was to make a Winnie the Pooh from McCall's pattern for her daughter Kim, then aged 4. It seems that an aggressive playmate walked off with her commercially made Winnie, so Mom calmed her down with the promise of a new one. Employing a terry cloth towel for his plush, and stuffing him with nylon stockings, he was ready to bring comfort and companionship to a little girl. With an 8 year-old brother close at hand, Mom decided to expand her project to include an Eeyore made from a gray wool skirt. This hand made Winnie was more closely guarded, and he has survived to this day. When son Terry came of age and headed off for Michigan State University, he left specific instructions to "get rid of all this kid stuff." But with three older children, Doris had been down this path before, and she quietly tucked the playthings away. During a visit home well into his second semester, young Terry asked if his Eeyore was still around. When it was produced for his inspection, he mumbled something about hanging on to it for one of the grandchildren to play with, and placed it in the center of his bed.

The Carrousel Museum Collection contains several versions of Winnie the Pooh, but none more delightful than a Pooh made by the German firm of Schuco. He measures 10in (25.4cm) high in a seated position, which is the only position he can assume since he is not jointed. He is made with a beautiful golden mohair, and his head is movable, held to the body with several strands of strong thread or cord. This method of creating movable parts is not new, and was employed by many makers to avoid the more costly and time consuming traditional method of making joints employing fibre discs held together with a cotter pin.

The Schuco Winnie was originally made under the license of Walt Disney Productions, and was introduced at Disneyland in the mid-1970s when the Disney movie of Winnie the Pooh was shown for the first time. The Schuco Pooh sold for a handsome price when he was new, and the value has appreciated greatly, as he is sought after by arctophiles everywhere. The Winnie display is complimented by an early Parker Brothers Winnie the Pooh game.

Winnie the Pooh, licensed by Disney, made by Schuco. Mohair. 10in (25.4cm).

Schuco's Winnie the Pooh visits Pooh and Eeyore made by Doris Michaud in 1968.

A Sweet Bear In Every Respect

Here we go with another bear from England story. If it is beginning to sound like I am an authority on England, I must confess that in the trips the Michauds have made to Britain, I have not once made the trip with them. My knowledge comes from the stories they have related, and some study on the subject I have done in my spare time. It seems that every time there is talk of another trip abroad, I put on my best "why not take me with you" look, but then I am placed in charge of looking after the bears at home. It's a heavy responsibility, and as the senior member of the group, I am most suited for the task. It would be nice, though, just once to visit all of the marvelous places they have talked about. But enough about that. Back to the story.

6in (15.2cm) German candy container.

One of the most unusual Teddies in the Carrousel Collection was discovered at a doll show in London. It was getting on toward the end of their two week tour, and the Michauds had made the rounds of the usual markets and shops. Fortunately they had made arrangements on this trip to stay in a Bed and Breakfast arrangement operated by Sarah and Colin Baddiel, two very wonderful Britains who operate a full time antique toy and book business in central London. An ad placed in the *Antique Toy World,* published in Chicago, Illinois, led the Michauds to the Baddiels, and they hit it off just marvelously.

Every room in their warm, friendly home was filled with the most exciting collection of antique toys (Colin's passion) and many rare examples of Golfiana. Sarah is one of only a handful of ladies in the world that are expert on the subject of golfing. Since the sport was invented in Scotland, it seems quite natural that a Britain would be an expert in this area. There were literally hundreds of marvelous items of golfing memorabilia on display, along with Sarah's impressive collection of books on the subject of juvenilia. About the only thing not collected by this charming couple was Teddy Bears! However, I suspect Terry and Doris may have remedied that before they left.

One of the additional bonuses in staying with people in the antique toy field was the information gleaned from them on where to hunt for treasures. They took the Michauds to markets and shops not normally attended by tourists from the "colonies." One such place was a small doll show held in a London hotel. By the time our dedicated hunters arrived, the line was already winding down a hallway and spilling into the lobby. Terry was certain that by the time they got in all the desirable Teddies would have long since been picked up by dealers and by the line of people ahead of them who, Terry was convinced, were all there to buy Teddy Bears!

That was probably only partially true, because Teddy Bear collecting has only recently come into its own in England, making it somewhat more difficult for today's arctophiles to find treasures there. At any rate, the long que (or lineup to Americans) finally diminished, and in went our eager couple. A tattered and worn bear from the 1950s was spotted here and there, and even a few earlier examples, bearing price tags to discourage early buyers. "But what's this curious little thing?" Doris wondered, as she picked up what was to be one of the rarest finds of their trip.

It appeared to be a squat little mohair bear with fixed position arms and legs, and a head that tilted off the body, held fast by a few stout threads. It had a removable metal lid under the head, which opened to reveal a tin cylindrical container under it. On the bottom the metal can was stamped "ORIGI ges. gesch reg."

The dealer knew nothing of this little bear, and was somewhat reluctant to sell it, pending more information. However, a hefty sum of pounds Sterling was exchanged, and our little bear came back to Michigan. Subsequent investigation has led to the discovery that this small bear was actually a German candy container, and a German lady remembered him as having a ruff around the neck, which Doris has added. His head is held in place by a magnet.

Imagine the delight of a child opening this bear to discover a cache of tasty morsels. It can't possibly compare, however, to the delight Doris experienced in discovering this German candy container.

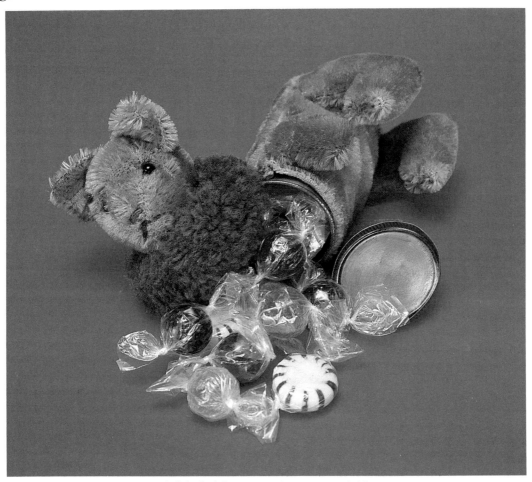

A delightful surprise for a 1920s child.

Teddy Wears The Fashion Of The Day

The Carrousel Museum Collection has been built over many years using a variety of means to acquire the bears. Travel has played an important role in assembling many of the Teddies, but one very simple and low cost method has been employed by the Michauds on a number of occasions successfully. It's the classified ad.

For a very small cost, classified ads can be placed in your local newspapers. Probably another related area that is over-looked by arctophiles are the small weekly papers that serve a rural and small community readership. These ads are even less expensive, and can occasionally strike a response with a reader. To concentrate on vintage Teddies, Terry and Doris usually specify they are interested in bears 40 years of age or older.

Such an ad placed in a shopper's guide that serves central Michigan produced a very special Teddy in the late 1970s. A woman read the ad and wrote to the Michauds to tell them of a Teddy she had for sale, and she enclosed a picture. The photo did not show much detail, but the price asked was reasonable, so Doris wrote back to the correspondent and enclosed a check, asking her to include any details regarding her or the bear that might be of interest.

Within a week a small package arrived, containing a well worn 13in (33cm) jointed Teddy, wearing a yellow knit sweater and a pair of overalls. The enclosed letter explained that the woman's parents owned a hardware store in a small village, where they sold software as well as hardware. Since it was a farming community, one of the more popular items in the store was their line of Lee overalls. The lady went on to say that she recalls playing in the store as a young girl, and one day the Lee overall salesman came in with a gift for her. It was a delightful small Teddy Bear, who proudly wore Lee overalls. The sweater was added by the lady's mother at a later date.

Were the overalls a salesman's sample? Did the salesman have them specially made? Did the company make a line of clothing for dolls? Answers to these questions will probably never be known, but you can be sure that this bear is as cherished today in the Carrousel Collection as it was cherished by a little girl who received it in the 1920s.

OPPOSITE PAGE: Passing the time of day at the store.

Just Ted

If a contest were held just among the Carrousel Collection, with ribbons awarded for various categories, it would be difficult at best to choose winners. I would like to believe that I might take the title for the most intelligent, but the Librarian and perhaps a few others might challenge that claim. There would certainly be a host of candidates for Most Loved, Tallest, Shortest, Best Classic Look, and so on. However, I can really only think of one contender for the category of Teddy Bear With the Most Character. That is not to imply that there is not an abundance of Teddies with character amongst us, but I'm certain that the title would be won hands down by Just Ted.

This one of a kind Teddy Bear came into the family back in 1976. Terry and Doris were set up at one of Carol Morse's popular antique mall shows in Flint, Michigan. During the course of the last day of the show, a well dressed gentleman passed by the booth rather slowly, carefully studying everything. I was standing erect on the top shelf with my sign declaring an interest in old Teddy Bears, and I thought at first that he was quite taken with me, but looking back on the situation, I'm reasonably certain it was the sign I was holding that held his attention.

He had a paper bag cradled under one arm, and after some hesitation, he stepped forward and inquired "Do you folks think you might be interested in my Bear?" Terry and Doris pressed forward and peered into the now open bag, and staring up at them with a great look of anticipation was a Teddy Bear with such charm and character that even I have to admit to a fleeting moment of envy. "He's really great," was Terry's enthusiastic response. "Did he have a name?" "Just Ted," the man stated matter-of-factly. "Any idea how old he is?" Terry inquired. "Of course," the gentleman responded, "we were twins, you know!"

Just Ted stands 18in (45.7cm) tall, with long grey mohair, black stitched nose and claws, and black shoe button eyes. His most outstanding characteristics are his ears, with the left ear standing erect and the right ear sagging toward the shoulder. The question frequently asked when the Michauds share Just Ted's story is, "How could anyone part with their very own Teddy Bear?" After having acquired a number of Teddies from their original owners, Terry and Doris have come to the conclusion that with people such as Just Ted's owner, there is an underlying concern for Teddy's eventual fate. The strong love and affection the Michauds show for the bears in their keeping had undoubtedly convinced a number of people that they have made the right decision.

Just Ted has such strong appeal that he was given the honor of being the first Teddy in the series of recreations from the Carrousel Museum Collection. He was introduced in the spring of 1984, and he quickly achieved the title of Best Selling Bear in the Carrousel line.

The challenge is before me now, as I was selected as the second Teddy to be recreated in this series. I'm most pleased that the Michauds not only selected 100% mohair for my recreation, but they make special glasses for my clone as well. I must admit to being a little nervous about going head to head with a bear that has the instant appeal that Just Ted has. He may be cute, but he doesn't have a book to his credit.

LEFT: Just Ted, a 1924 grey mohair Teddy Bear. 18in (45.7cm).

OPPOSITE PAGE: My, what a distinctive profile!

In Conclusion: Carrousel Teddy Bears —

Terry and Doris Michaud's unique background of nearly 20 years in the antique toy and doll business made it a natural progression to collecting Teddy Bears. The Carrousel Museum Collection is widely recognized by leading authorities as one of the most significant collections in the country. The Michauds accepted a challenge in 1978 to design and produce a handcrafted Teddy Bear that incorporated all of the desirable characteristics of their antique Teddy Bears. It was a challenge that was to take two years and hundreds of frustrating hours of trial and error. One of their earliest Teddies reached the hands of the late Peter Bull, who encouraged them to continue.

The first commercial offering made its debut on the east coast in 1980. Today, the Michauds' handcrafted Teddy Bears are offered by over 100 leading shops from coast to coast. Doris and Terry take great pride in their Teddies, which have won numerous awards and are highly prized by collectors everywhere. All are fully jointed, with glass eyes and hump back, just like the original Teddy Bears. Added to their original designs are recreations of some of the more enchanting Teddy Bears in the museum collection.

Limited assistance in cutting and sewing parts is utilized, but all finish work is accomplished by their family, with every bear receiving final touches by Doris. This personal assurance of quality will keep the Michauds' handcrafted Teddy Bears in great demand for years to come.

LEFT: *Terry and Doris Michaud with Just Ted original and their recreation.*

RIGHT: *Four Carrousel creations. Left to right: Ted the Good News Bear'r; Sir Edward II; Baby Edward; and Brother Theodore.*

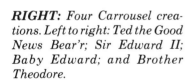

The author with his Carrousel recreation.